T0140827

Studien zur Mustererkennung

herausgegeben von:

Prof. Dr.-Ing. Heinrich Niemann
Prof. Dr.-Ing. Elmar Nöth

Bibliografische Information der Deutschen Nationalbibliothek

Die Deutsche Nationalbibliothek verzeichnet diese Publikation in der Deutschen Nationalbibliografie; detaillierte bibliografische Daten sind im Internet über http://dnb.d-nb.de abrufbar.

©Copyright Logos Verlag Berlin GmbH 2018
Alle Rechte vorbehalten.

ISBN 978-3-8325-4827-8
ISSN 1617-0695

Logos Verlag Berlin GmbH
Comeniushof
Gubener Str. 47
10243 Berlin
Tel.: +49 030 42 85 10 90
Fax: +49 030 42 85 10 92
INTERNET: http://www.logos-verlag.de

Probabilistic Fusion of Multiple Distributed Sensors

DISSERTATION

zur Erlangung des Grades eines Doktors
der Ingenieurwissenschaften

vorgelegt von

M. Sc. Lukas Köping

geb. am 16.05.1984 in Posen

eingereicht bei der Naturwissenschaftlich-Technischen Fakultät

der Universität Siegen

Siegen 2018

Betreuer und erster Gutachter

Prof. Dr.-Ing. Marcin Grzegorzek
Universität Siegen

Zweiter Gutachter

Prof. Dr.-Ing. Frank Deinzer

Hochschule für angewandte Wissenschaften
Würzburg - Schweinfurt

Tag der mündlichen Prüfung

07. September 2018

Acknowledgements

This thesis summarises the main results of my work as a PhD student during my time at the University of Applied Sciences in Würzburg and at the Research Group for Pattern Recognition at the University of Siegen. Here, I want to say thank you to everyone that supported me during this period of my life.

I wish to thank my first supervisor Prof. Dr.-Ing. Marcin Grzegorzek who guided me with his advice through my research and my career. I have not only learned from you as a technical advisor, but was always impressed by your positive thinking and view of the world which helped me especially in difficult situations. I want to express my special appreciation to my second supervisor Prof. Dr.-Ing. Frank Deinzer who has been supportive since my days as undergraduate. Thank you for introducing and guiding me through the world of science. The lessons I have learned from this journey will always be an invaluable experience.

I would also like to gratefully acknowledge the patient supervision and collaboration with Dr. Kimiaki Shirahama. I am grateful to all my colleagues of the Research Group of Pattern Recognition at the University of Siegen, my colleagues at the University of Applied Sciences in Würzburg and the GEIST research group at the AGH University of Science and Technology in Krakow. Thanks to to all my research colleagues of the research training group GRK 1564 "Imaging New Modalities". I did not only enjoy the scientific discussions with you, but also the time outside of the laboratories. I am thankful to the financial support of the German Federal Ministry of Education and Research (BMBF). I also want to thank all my Bachelor and Master students who wrote their thesis under my supervision. I hope you learned as much from me as I did from you.

This work would not have been possible without the support of my parents, Lucyna and Waldemar Köping, and my wife Maria Köping. Thank you very much for your patience and thoughtfulness during this long and not always easy period of time.

Lukas Köping

Abstract

The human perception of the environment is largely determined by the fact that a large number of sensory impressions are recorded and processed simultaneously. In particular, the combination of these individual information ensures that the brain is able to resolve perceptual ambiguities. In the present work applications are shown, in which a multitude of different sensors are fused. Most of the used sensors come from wearable devices such as smartphones or smartwatches. In the area of activity detection, the data is used to determine a person's current activity. For this purpose, a method based on the creation of a codebook is presented that extracts characteristic features for the later use in a classification algorithm from the incoming time series data. This significantly shortens the laborious step of manual feature extraction. Various experiments validate that this method achieves results comparable to the state-of-the-art. Compared to many other feature learning methods the codebook-based approach only requires very few intuitively tunable parameters, so that a simple and fast implementation is possible. In addition, it is embedded into an easily extendible general framework for human activity recognition.

Another application for sensor fusion is indoor localisation. Due to the strong signal attenuation, satellite-supported navigation systems can hardly be used inside buildings. The system introduced here fuses data from accelerometers, gyroscopes, barometers and Wi-Fi measurements to track the position of a person inside a building. The data is processed using recursive density estimation. For this, the state, the transition probability and observation models must be developed appropriately. The result of this process is a probability density over the estimated state space for each time of the estimation. In the context of this work, various statistical models are presented which allow to integrate data that represents human movement patterns. In particular, these are used as additional information for the statistical state estimation.

Finally, a gesture recognition system is presented that uses recursive density estimation to classify gestures. By including the pattern class as part of the state, a probability density can be specified for all classes based on the incoming sensor values. As a basis for comparison, average sequences are calculated from previously recorded training data.

Zusammenfassung

Die menschliche Wahrnehmung der Umwelt ist maßgeblich dadurch bestimmt, dass eine Vielzahl von Sinneseindrücken gleichzeitig aufgenommen und verarbeitet werden. Insbesondere die Kombination der einzelnen Informationen sorgt dafür, dass auftretende Mehrdeutigkeiten vom Gehirn aufgelöst werden können. In der vorliegenden Arbeit werden unterschiedliche Anwendungsfälle aufgezeigt, in denen eine Vielzahl unterschiedlicher Sensorik miteinander kombiniert werden. Die verwendetete Sensorik stammt dabei aus handelsüblichen tragbaren Geräten wie Smartphones oder Smartwatches. Im Bereich der Aktivitätenerkennung werden die Daten dazu verwendet, um die aktuelle Aktivität einer Person bestimmen zu können. Hierfür wird ein auf der Erstellung eines Codebuchs basierendes Verfahren vorgestellt, das charakteristische Merkmale für den Klassifikationsalgorithmus selbstständig aus den Zeitdaten der Sensoren extrahiert. Damit lässt sich der arbeitsaufwendige Schritt der manuellen Merkmalsextraktion signifikant verkürzen. Die experimentellen Ergebnisse zeigen dabei auf, dass dieses Verfahren mit dem Stand der Technik vergleichbare und teilweise bessere Resultate erzielt. Im Vergleich zu vielen anderen Verfahren zum Erlernen von Merkmalen kommt das hier Vorgestellte mit sehr wenigen Parametern aus, so dass eine einfache und schnelle Implementierung möglich ist. Zudem wird es in ein allgemeines und einfach zu erweiterndes Rahmenwerk eingebettet.

Als weiterer Anwendungsfall für die Sensorfusion wird ein Indoorlokalisierungssystem vorgestellt. Aufgrund der starken Signalabschwächung können satellitengestütze Navigationssysteme im Inneren eines Gebäudes kaum verwendet werden. Das hier vorgestellte System fusioniert u.a. die Daten von Beschleunigungssensoren, Gyroskopen, Barometern und Wi-Fi Messungen, um die Position einer Person im Gebäudeinneren mitverfolgen zu können. Die Daten werden dabei im Rahmen einer rekursiven Dichteschätzung verarbeitet. Hierfür muss der Zustandsraum, die Systemübergangs- und Beobachtungswahrscheinlichkeiten geeignet modelliert werden. Das Ergebnis dieses Prozesses ist eine Wahrscheinlichkeitsdichte über den Zustandsraum für jeden Zeitpunkt der Schätzung. Im Rahmen dieser Arbeit werden insbesondere verschiedene statistische Modelle aufgezeigt, die die Integration der Beschleunigungsdaten erlauben. Diese werden in menschliche Bewegungsmuster umgewandelt und fließen als zusätzliche Informationen in die statistische Schätzung ein.

Zuletzt wird ein Gestenerkennungssystem vorgestellt, das die Klassifikation anhand einer Dichteschätzung vornimmt. Indem die Musterklasse in den zu schätzenden Zustand aufgenommen wird, kann anhand der eingehenden Sensortwerte eine Wahrscheinlichkeitsdichte für alle Klassen angegeben werden. Als Vergleichsgrundlage werden aus zuvor aufgenommenen Trainingsdaten durchschnittliche Sequenzen berechnet.

Contents

List of Figures

List of Tables

Chapter 1

Introduction

Humans perceive their surrounding environment by processing the input of multiple senses like vision, hearing, taste, smell and touch (see Fig. 1.1). These sensory impressions are detected by eyes, ears, skin and other sensory organs, transformed into electrical impulses and finally transferred to the brain where they are combined and analysed. Only this combination of many complementary information sources allows the brain to create a complete picture of the environment and, especially, the ability to resolve ambiguities in the perception of the environment. An example for this is a study about the speech detection threshold which is defined as the quietest sound that can still be understood by a person. In the early 2000s, a number of experiments were conducted that indicate that seeing a speaker's lips and face motion reduces the speech detection threshold of the listener by around 1 - 3 dB [89, 88] and helps to increase the overall intelligibility of the spoken words [217]. Nevertheless, in which way the brain fuses all information and concludes an ambiguous situation is still under active research. One hypothesis is that it relies on a mechanism that is similar to a Bayesian model

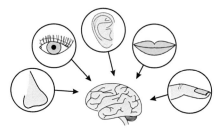

Figure 1.1: Every single human sense delivers important inputs that are fused in the brain into a complete picture of the environment.

Figure 1.2: Example of wearable devices. The devices are equipped with sensors like accelerometer, gyroscope, barometer, Wi-Fi, galvanic skin sensor and electrooculography.

with a maximum likelihood estimation, where past experiences are reflected as prior knowledge [126, 68]. This prior knowledge is used to exclude certain solutions, which do not coincide with past experiences, from the outset. Thereby, prior knowledge is built up over the complete life time and can be seen as model of the brain of how things work in the world. The brain then recognizes such situations and applies its experience to it.

It is also important to mention that the estimation of reality becomes more and more accurate with an increasing number of sensory impressions. An example of this is an approaching car. The mere still image would tell the observer little about the actual speed of the vehicle. The integration of observations over a longer period of time, however, allows to estimate exactly how fast the vehicle is moving. This means that the human being does continuously integrate previous knowledge into his estimation of reality.

1.1 Sensors

In a technical world, human senses are replaced by a variety of sensors, while computers and algorithms take over the task of the brain. The focus in this thesis lies on sensors that are provided within commodity hardware like smartphones, smartwatches and smartglasses (see Fig. 1.2). Following, most commonly found sensors are described in more detail:

- **Accelerometer** The accelerometer was one of the earliest sensors that was adopted in wearable devices. It measures the change of velocity over time, $\frac{\Delta v}{\Delta t}$, in each of the three directions x, y and z. The accelerometer signal is especially useful for detecting any kind of motions of the device and ultimately of the user.

An extension to the accelerometer is the linear accelerometer. Since earth's gravity is a constant force that can be measured by an accelerometer, it also overlies the user's movement signal. To avoid this, the gravity vector is subtracted from the acceleration so that all measurements directly reflect movements.

- **Gyroscope** In addition to accelerometers, gyroscopes measure the change of rotational velocity for each axis in $\frac{rad}{s}$, so that the combination of accelerometer and gyroscope makes movement changes recognisable in six different dimensions.

- **Magnetometer** Magnetometers measure the magnetic field around the device and are used in smartphones as substitute for traditional compasses. Due to their sensitiveness to surrounding electrical fields, especially indoors, these sensors can be highly effected by noise.

  Together, the accelerometer, gyroscope and magnetometer form the Inertial Measurement Unit (IMU), which is traditionally used for navigation purely based on the detection of movement.

- **Barometer** A barometer is a measurement device to determine the Earth's atmospheric pressure. Since there is a physical correlation between detected pressure and altitude, a barometer is suitable for height estimation.

- **Gravity sensor** Deviated from the accelerometer sensor, a gravity sensor measures the influence of the earth's gravity force on each of the three axis. Often, the gravity sensor is not a dedicated hardware sensor, but instead the result of a fusion process of the accelerometer, gyroscope and magnetometer.

- **Electrooculography (EOG)** Known from the medical sector, EOG is a sensor that was just recently implemented in wearable devices. EOG is based on the observation that human eyes act like a dipole. Therefore, every movement of the eye causes small measurable changes in the electrical potential which is recognised by an EOG. Based on this signal, various eye-based activities and physical conditions can be detected. For example, it is well known that a high eye-blinking frequency is an indicator for drowsiness. Applications can be found mainly in the automotive industry with the aim to identify exhausted car and truck drivers.

  Bulling [32] has shown in his work that by applying sophisticated feature engineering to EOG data he is able to detect activities like reading, typing, browsing the web or watching a video (see Fig. 1.3).

- **Heart Rate** Heart rate sensors can be found in smartwatches or fitness trackers and work on the basis of the absorption of infrared light by the blood stream. At

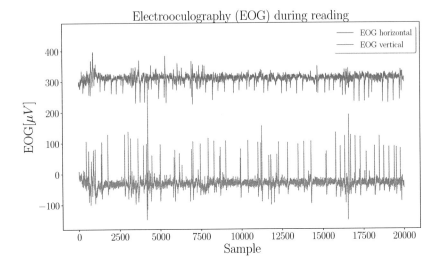

Figure 1.3: The electrooculography (EOG) signal is shown for the horizontal and vertical direction of the eye movement while the user was reading an article on a website. In the horizontal signal every sharp minimum is associated with the end of a line and a jumping back to the beginning of the next line. The peaks in the vertical signal are mainly caused by eye blinks.

the beginning, heart rate measurements were mostly used by athletes for monitoring their current pulse level for training purposes. However, with the proliferation of this sensor into everyday devices, it can help to measure the overall health status of a person. The special usefulness comes from the fact that people are wearing smartwatches all day long, which in turn means that the heart rate gets monitored over a long period of time. This has various advantages compared to the single measurements, when people are visiting the doctor once in a while.

- **Galvanic Skin Conductance** Galvanic Skin Conductance/Response, also known as electro-dermal activity, measures the electric conductibility of the human skin. In particular, there exists a relation between the amount of sweat and the conductivity of the skin. Since sweating can be triggered by the vegetative nervous system, it is an indicator for the emotional stress a person is suffering from.

1.2 Applications

This dissertation deals with the general problem of extracting meaningful information from time series data that are obtained by multiple sensors. This work picks out two different problems in which time series occur and those will be treated in more detail: Activity recognition and indoor localisation. Although time series play an essential role in both problems, the approaches to solve them are very different. Activitiy recognition is essentially a classification problem, whereas in indoor localisation a state must be estimated over a longer period of time. Next, both problems should be introduced briefly.

1.2.1 Activity Recognition

One way of extracting information from wearable devices' sensor data is found in the area of activity recognition. Here, the goal is to derive the activity a person is currently performing from the sensor data that is collected with wearable devices [142, 42]. Examples of such activities include basic movements like running or sitting but also include complex activities like cooking or going shopping.

Activity Recognition became an important research topic in the last years due to various reasons. Every new wearable device includes an increasing number of sensors which eases the task of data collection. Secondly, there is currently a trend for a "Quantified Self", so that people are more and more interested in tracking their daily activities to optimise their lifestyle. At the same time, this approach can also be used in the health care sector. Hereby, a special target is the sector of elderly care which becomes of increasing importance due to the current age structure in most Western industrial countries. The goal is to support elderly care with intelligent systems, so that caregivers can be relieved [186].

Besides the detection of physical activities, also affective computing [198], which can be described as emotional activity recognition, gains importance. The main driver for this field of research is the notion that machines will only be recognised as "intelligent" if they are able to understand the user's feelings. Again, many of the aforementioned sensors like the heartbeat sensor or the detection of galvanic skin conductance can be employed in a system that is able to recognise the user's current emotional state.

Finally, a smaller part of the thesis is also dedicated to the problem of sensor-based gesture recognition. Gesture recognition can be seen as a subset of the activity recognition problem since it also performs classification based on streaming sensor data provided by an action of the user. However, gestures also have internal parameters like the intensity with which the gesture is performed. For example, an intense shaking of

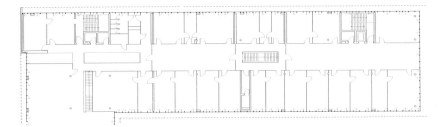

Figure 1.4: One of the contributions in this thesis is an indoor localisation system based on the previously described sensors. The sensor data is fused together with map information in a recursive density framework for which particle filters are used as implementation.

the head has to be interpreted differently than a slight shaking of the head. Algorithms for gesture recognition have to be stable against such variations.

1.2.2   Indoor Localisation

Within buildings, there are hardly any possibilities to determine or even track one's own position with technical systems. The main problem here is that the well-known GPS signal cannot be received inside buildings. To overcome this problem, sensors like accelerometers, gyroscopes and magnetometers can be utilised to transfer the principle of inertial navigation into the indoor area. However, as will be shown, these sensors alone are not accurate enough, so that other information, especially Wi-Fi, should be integrated.

Historically, indoor localisation has already been applied in the robotics area [57, 230]. Nevertheless, there are many differences between robotic navigation and indoor localisation for persons: (i) Robots are typically equipped with more sophisticated sensors like Lidar (light detection and ranging) or different camera systems. Contrary, humans typically only carry wearable devices with low-cost sensors. (ii) Sensors are fixed in known positions on the robot and thus also never change in their orientation. The main purpose of wearable devices usually is not activity recognition or indoor localisation. This causes a permanent position and orientation change as the user interacts with the device. (iii) Usually, the direction of the robot's movement is clear since an internal control unit issues this movement command which makes future states of the robot more predictable. On the other hand, humans' movements can be sometimes unforeseeable. For example, he might not follow a proposed path, suddenly turn around or meet a person he wants to talk to. All these situations are typically not predictable.

1.3 Motivation

One of the key points in Mark Weiser's vision of Ubiquitous Computing [253] are intelligent machines that disappear from the conscious perception of the user. To enable such intelligent human-computer interacting systems, context is one of the main components. As described by [2], context can conceptually be defined as any information that helps to characterise a current situation. Thereby, location and the user's current activity play a major role [234]. However, both areas are under active research due to various challenges that can be found:

- **Feature extraction from time series data** Feature extraction is an important step during the creation of Machine Learning systems. However, finding features that are able to discriminate between different classes often requires a deep understanding of the underlying problem. This makes it difficult to transfer existing solutions to new problems. On the other hand, current research in Deep Artificial Neural Networks (Deep Learning) has shown to be able to automatically extract representative features with which state-of-the-art classification results are possible. The main drawback of Deep Learning, however, is that it requires setting up an appropriate network architecture and the associated large amount of parameters that must be set either by experience or experimentation. Despite the success of neural networks, many problems often can be solved with simpler methods. One goal in this work is to provide a method that goes without the need for domain knowledge and at the same time is easy to set up, implement and applicable to a wide area of sensors.

- **Data labelling in activity recognition** Labelling data in activity recognition is laborious and highly time-consuming. Nevertheless, labelled data is of fundamental importance in supervised learning. Classification algorithms in activity recognition should reduce the amount of work that must be put into the labelling of data.

- **Extensibility of activity recognition systems** As described in earlier sections, wearable devices are equipped with an increasing number of sensor modalities. In addition, users often carry several devices with them at the same time. In order to combine sensors of different devices, a framework is necessary that collects and fuses data in a common place. Such a framework should be easily extendible and should be able to cope with different sensor modalities and their specific characteristics like different measurement units or frequency of recording.

- **Indoor location estimation** It is easy to track the position outside using the GPS satellite system. However, as soon as a person enters a building, it is currently not possible to further track his position. A functioning indoor localisation system would be a key enabler for many different applications in security, health care, emergency services or visitor navigation [97].

- **Latency free system response** Interactions with a system should not be negatively affected by long breaks between the input of the user and the system's response. In an optimal case, a system already knows the intention of the user even before he finishes his input.

- **Gesture spotting** Interactive systems should be able to recognize gestures without the user having to explicitly inform the system about the beginning of a new gesture. This ability is called "gesture spotting" and is essential if the user wants to interact with a system in a natural way.

1.4   Contribution

To address the described challenges the main contributions presented in this dissertation can be split into the following categories:

- **Feature learning for time series data** A feature learning method is proposed that extracts representative features from time series data without the need to take specifics of the underlying application or domain knowledge into consideration. The method can be easily optimised since it requires only a small number of intuitive parameters. The features are learned on an unlabelled set of data and are then used in a Support Vector Machine for classification. The training of the classifier can be carried out with loosely labelled data. These are time sequences that contain a certain activity, but it is possible that other activities are also present in the same sequence.

- **General framework for activity recognition** The introduced feature learning method is used to build a general framework for activity recognition. This framework allows to use an arbitrary number of sensors as long as the sensor outputs are time series data. The data transfer and synchronisation of the data is handled by an open protocol.

- **Indoor localisation system** An indoor localisation system is introduced in which different sensors are fused in a recursive density estimation framework, implemented by particle filtering. The walking behaviour of a user is modelled by taking map information into consideration. Estimated positions are evaluated probabilistically by combining different sensors outputs.

- **Statistical models for indoor localisation** All implemented sensors require a statistical model to be integrated into the localisation system. Models contributed by the author include the evaluation of the user's walking behaviour by the step the user made, asking the user for feedback and estimating the walking direction. The latter model is supplemented by a mechanism that discards measurements that are likely to be erroneous. In addition, a user's locomotion is distinguished into one of several possible classes and the result is integrated into the statistical model.

- **Gesture recognition system** A combination of state estimation and classification is proposed in the context of gesture recognition. The system is able to spot a gesture in a stream of sensor data without additional help. Many other systems in the literature need an explicit start signal to mark the beginning of a gesture. In addition, the system is able to classify gestures before they have been completed by the user. This can be used to realize interactive applications with low latencies. Finally, parameters such as the speed at which the gesture is executed can also be determined.

1.5   Overview

The outline of the theses is as follows: Chapter 2 gives an overview over basic concepts of pattern recognition and introduces the mathematical notation used throughout this work. After that, time series classification and general state-of-the-art methods to solve these types of problems are introduced. Activity recognition as one application in time series classification is presented together with its problem-specific characteristics.

In chapter 3, a method is proposed that extracts features from multi-dimensional time series data without manual intervention and with only a few intuitively tunable hyper-parameters. Additionally, a general framework for activity recognition is proposed.

Next, chapter 4 introduces recursive density estimation and particle filtering as a method to fuse multiple sensors over time. This is applied to indoor localisation where different statistical models are explained that integrate the sensors into the framework. The chapter closes with the application of multiple sensors in gesture recognition. Here, the classification and state estimation are combined in a single framework.

The proposed methods are experimentally evaluated in chapter 5, while chapter 6 closes this dissertation with a summary and possibilities to extend the presented work in the future.

Chapter 2

Pattern Recognition for Time Series Data

This chapter introduces concepts for the recognition of patterns in time series data. First, a general overview of the basic pattern recognition pipeline is given. In conjunction with this, the mathematical notation used throughout this thesis will be presented. Following, time series data as a special form of data as well as traditional techniques for time series classification are introduced. This includes feature-based and distance-based methods. The chapter closes with activity recognition as one domain for time series classification problems. Here, different properties of activity recognition that currently make this field so interesting for research will be shown.

2.1 Pattern Recognition

The goal of a pattern recognition system is to automatically identify and extract patterns in data using technical and mathematical methods [181]. Hereby, one of the most important pattern recognition tasks is *classification* where a pattern is categorised into one of several "meaningful" classes. However, what is defined as meaningful always depends on the underlying use case and domain. For example, in the medical field, pixels in an X-ray image can be classified into healthy and diseased tissue. In speech recognition, audio signals are broken down into individual words, where each word can represent an own class. In this work, the main focus lies in the recognition of daily physical activities of humans like walking, sitting or lying down. The data that are used for this task come from sensors like accelerometers, gyroscopes and magnetometers. These sensors are typically found in commercially available devices such as smartphones, smartwatches or smartglasses.

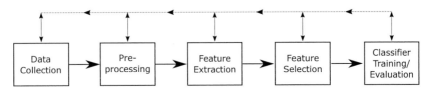

Figure 2.1: The general pattern recognition pipeline (Figure adapted from [229]). After collection and preprocessing of data, features are extracted from which a best subset is chosen. In a final step a classifier is trained and evaluated. The results from this evaluation are fed back to the system and optimised until the best classification results are achieved.

2.1.1   Pattern recognition pipeline

For pattern recognition a generic pipeline (see Fig. 2.1) has gained acceptance that describes the path from the initial sensor data acquisition to the final classification [229, 181]. In an initial data collection step, data is acquired that will be utilised for the specific use case. As indicated above, the data might be collected with sensors like cameras, microphones or accelerometers. Next, the raw sensor data is preprocessed. Common goals of this step are noise removal, segmentation of relevant parts from the background or normalisation of the input data, e.g. resizing, z-normalisation or re-orientation. In the feature extraction step characteristic descriptions of the data have to be found. This step has a key role in the pipeline and will be in the focus of this thesis. Using the extracted features should make it possible to distinguish different classes from each other, while at the same time the raw sensor data is transformed into a reduced representation. This is particularly important in areas in which raw data requires large amount of memory, e.g. image, video or time series data. Consequently, good features concentrate on the main part of the data for the underlying classification task, and therefore remove unnecessary parts of it. Automating this step in the pipeline currently belongs to the most widely researched areas in Machine Learning. Also in this thesis an automatic feature extraction method will be proposed in the upcoming chapter. In the feature selection step a subset of the initially extracted features is picked out. The selected features usually are the ones that are contributing the most to the final classification. In a final step, a classifier is trained and evaluated based on the extracted features. The result of this evaluation is the basis for further improvements of the system. All steps are iteratively repeated until the best classification result is achieved. Following, a more detailed look at the importance of features and the mechanism of a classifier is taken.

2.1.2 Classification

More formally, for a given problem the set of all relevant pattern classes is denoted as

$$\Omega = \{\Omega_1, \Omega_2, \Omega_3, \ldots, \Omega_k, \ldots, \Omega_\kappa\} \quad , \tag{2.1}$$

where each label Ω_k represents a single class.

A d-dimensional feature vector is denoted as $\mathbf{c}$. Each dimension of $\mathbf{c}$ corresponds to a singe feature c_ϑ, so that

$$\mathbf{c} = (c_1, c_2, c_3, \ldots, c_\vartheta, \ldots, c_d)^T, \quad c_\vartheta \in \mathbb{R}, \mathbf{c} \in \mathbb{R}^d \quad , \tag{2.2}$$

where ^{T} denotes the transposed vector. With this, each pattern can be represented as a point in a d-dimensional feature space.

Given a feature vector $\mathbf{c}$, the goal is to build a classifier that can correctly assign a class Ω_κ to each point in the feature space. A classifier can be interpreted as a function $g(\cdot)$ whose input is a feature vector and whose output is one of the problem-related class labels Ω_k:

$$g(\mathbf{c}) = \Omega_k \quad \text{and} \quad \Omega_k \in \Omega, \; k \in \{1, \ldots, \kappa\} \text{ and } \mathbf{c} \in \mathbb{R}^d \quad . \tag{2.3}$$

Examples for classifiers are Bayesian classifiers, Neural Networks, Decision Trees and Random Forests, Nearest Neighbour classifiers and Support Vector Machines (SVM). However, due to the high variety of existing classification algorithms, the reader is referred to one of the standard textbooks, for example [229, 27, 63].

Despite this diversity of classification methods, they all follow the same principle. In a training phase the classifier is provided N_{train} feature vectors together with their corresponding class label. This set is denoted as labelled training set C_{train} and defined as

$$C_{\text{train}} = \{(\mathbf{c}^1, y_1), (\mathbf{c}^2, y_2), (\mathbf{c}^3, y_3), \ldots, (\mathbf{c}^i, y_i), \ldots, (\mathbf{c}^{N_{\text{train}}}, y_{N_{\text{train}}})\} \quad . \tag{2.4}$$

y_i is one of $\{1, \ldots, \kappa\}$ and references to a class label Ω_k. Thus, every tuple, called sample, of C_{train} describes one annotated point in the feature space. This approach is also called supervised learning.

Similar to the training set, a testing set C_{test} is defined, consisting of N_{test} samples. The testing set

$$C_{\text{test}} = \{(\mathbf{c}^1, y_1), (\mathbf{c}^2, y_2), (\mathbf{c}^3, y_3), \ldots, (\mathbf{c}^j, y_j), \ldots, (\mathbf{c}^{N_{\text{test}}}, y_{N_{\text{test}}})\} \tag{2.5}$$

is used to evaluate the performance of a classifier. Hereby, one common evaluation criterion is the accuracy of a classifier which is defined as the number of correctly assigned class labels in relation to the total number of evaluated examples. Given a trained classifier it is now possible to assign a class label to each future feature vector $\mathbf{c}$. The border between two classes is also known as the decision boundary. This is illustrated for a feature space that was separated by a linear and non-linear SVM in Fig. 2.2.

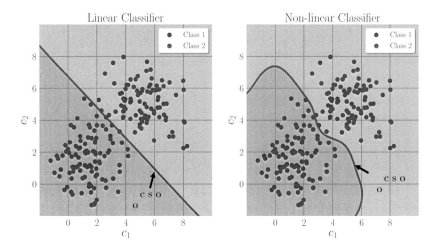

Figure 2.2: Example of two classifier that are learned one the same training set. On the left side the classifier is a linear SVM while on the right a non-linear SVM is used.

2.2 Time Series Classification

Time series analysis has been identified as one of the top ten challenges in data mining [259]. This is hardly a surprise, given the fact that time series appear in so many applications. A prime example here is speech recognition since speech is recorded as an acoustic signal [104, 15]. For a long time Hidden Markov Models (HMMs) [204] had been the most widely applied method, however, nowadays Deep Artificial Neural Networks dominate this field due to their ability to learn complex structures from large amounts of data [104, 143]. Very close to speech recognition is the area of music informatics in which the identification of similar pieces of music, genre and instrumental identification or mood prediction play a major role [108, 175, 174]. In the medical area, time signals can be found in the analysis of electroencephalograms (EEG) [3], electrocardiograms [4] (ECG) or the electromyograms (EMG)[197]. Driven by the miniaturization of sensors and the connection of these to the internet, the field of Internet of Things became increasingly important in the last years. And since most of the built-in sensors are measuring acceleration, temperature, humidity and other environmental factors over a period of time, time series analysis is applied there [228, 41]. A wider list of applications can be found in [141]. The focus in this thesis lies on time series data for human activity

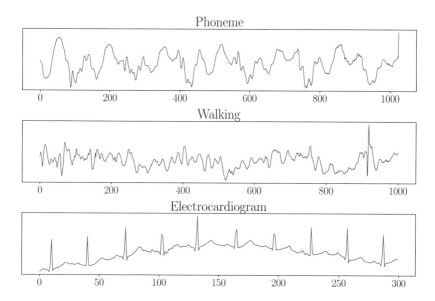

Figure 2.3: Examples for three different time series occurrences. At the top, a recorded phoneme [13, 96] is illustrated. Phonemes are used as basic building blocks within speech recognition. The image in the middle shows the accelerometer signal of a walking person, while the bottom image is an excerpt of a patient's electrocardiogram to measure the electric activity of the heart (MHEALTH dataset [17]).

recognition which are recorded by sensors like accelerometers or gyroscopes. Examples of different time signals are illustrated in Fig. 2.3.

Based on their nature, time series data have certain properties that separate them from other types of data:

- Time series are characterised by the fact that the data is a consecutive series of points for which the order is of importance [12] and thus, a single point usually cannot be considered in isolation. However, it is not clear, how much influence a point in the past has on current and future measurement values. Thus, it is extremely difficult to catch such dependencies.

- Due to the high frequency with which data are recorded, time series typically are considered as high-dimensional data. Assuming a sensor frequency of 100Hz leads to 6000 measurement points after a minute of recording. Since such high-dimensional data usually are not tractable for classification algorithms, the raw sensor signal is often transformed into a different representation. A more detailed view on this will be given in Sec. 2.2.2 and Sec. 2.2.3.

- Time series data often contain a significant amount of noise so that additional signal processing is needed as a preprocessing step. However, noise removal can produce undesired artefacts like lags in the filtered data [259] which in turn has to be considered when training a classifier.

- In addition, time series data is not stationary. Shifts of characteristics like the mean or the variance are not necessarily meaningful for the underlying classification problem [141]. Instead, their change might be caused by environmental factors that are not captured in the data.

2.2.1 Notation

In the previous section, the general methodology of pattern recognition was introduced. What follows next is a short description of the notation used throughout this work.

A series of sensor measurements $\mathbf{o}_{1:\tau}$ is defined as an ordered sequence of observations

$$\mathbf{o}_{1:\tau} = \left(o_1, \ldots, o_t, \ldots, o_\tau\right)^T \quad \text{with} \quad 1 < t < \tau \text{ and } t, \tau \in \mathbb{N} \tag{2.6}$$

that starts with the index 1 and ends with the index τ. If not otherwise stated, an observation is a single measurement point of a sensor. Often multiple sensors are used at the same time or a single sensor takes measurements across multiple dimension, e.g. the 3D space with its x, y and z-dimensions. In the latter case every measurement dimension is treated as a self-contained sensor. Given M different sensors, the observation series of the s-th sensor is denoted as

$$\mathbf{o}_{1:\tau_s}^s = \left(o_1^s, \ldots, o_t^s, \ldots, o_{\tau_s}^s\right)^T, \quad s \in \{1, .., M\} \ . \tag{2.7}$$

The superscript s will be omitted in further descriptions whenever it is not of importance that a specific sensor is meant. A multivariate time series consists of two or more series of sensor measurements that observe the same subject and will be denoted as

$$\mathbf{O}_{1:\tau} = \left(\mathbf{o}_{1:\tau_1}^1, \ldots, \mathbf{o}_{1:\tau_n}^n, \ldots \mathbf{o}_{1:\tau_M}^M\right)^T \ . \tag{2.8}$$

It should also be noted that the number of observations in all M observation series does not necessarily have to be equal, so that in general

$$\mid \mathbf{o}_{1:\tau_1}^1 \mid \neq \ldots \neq \mid \mathbf{o}_{1:\tau_s}^s \mid \neq \ldots \neq \mid \mathbf{o}_{1:\tau_M}^M \mid \ . \tag{2.9}$$

This is mainly due to the fact that each sensor records data at a specific frequency. A series of observations can be split into a shorter segment which will be denoted as

$$\mathbf{o}_{n:m}^s = \left(o_n^s, \ldots, o_t^s, \ldots, o_m^s\right)^T \quad \text{with} \quad 1 \leq n < m \leq \tau_s \ , \tag{2.10}$$

and which is a subset of the sequence $\mathbf{o}_{1:\tau_s}^s$.

Summarising, in supervised time series classification, the task becomes to assign a label y_i to a (multivariate) sequence of measurements. For this, a training set

$$C_{\text{train}} = \left\{ \left(\mathbf{O}_{1:\tau_1}^1, y_1\right), \left(\mathbf{O}_{1:\tau_2}^2, y_2\right), \left(\mathbf{O}_{1:\tau_3}^3, y_3\right), \ldots, \left(\mathbf{O}_{1:\tau_i}^i, y_i\right), \ldots, \left(\mathbf{O}_{1:\tau_{N_{\text{train}}}}^{N_{\text{train}}}, y_{N_{\text{train}}}\right) \right\} \tag{2.11}$$

and a testing set

$$C_{\text{test}} = \left\{ \left(\mathbf{O}_{1:\tau_1}^1, y_1\right), \left(\mathbf{O}_{1:\tau_2}^2, y_2\right), \left(\mathbf{O}_{1:\tau_3}^3, y_3\right), \ldots, \left(\mathbf{O}_{1:\tau_j}^j, y_j\right), \ldots, \left(\mathbf{O}_{1:\tau_{N_{\text{test}}}}^{N_{\text{test}}}, y_{N_{\text{test}}}\right) \right\} \tag{2.12}$$

are available.

2.2.2 Feature-based classification

In order to apply Machine Learning, methods like SVMs or Decision Trees need a feature vector together with the corresponding label as input. To be able to use these methods also for time series classification, the sequential data must firstly be transformed into such a feature vector. Following, some common techniques for this task are presented.

The simplest way to classify time series data is to use each data point as single feature in the feature vector $\mathbf{c}$, so that $\mathbf{c} = \mathbf{o}_{1:\tau}$. With this, a time series of length τ leads to a feature vector of dimensionality $\mathbb{R}^\tau$. Though, such an approach has some disadvantages that make its usage only applicable for the simplest cases. For one, each data point is considered in isolation from other data points. However, the interplay of consecutive data points usually plays a crucial role in time series data. In addition, if feature vectors are constructed in this way, their high-dimensionality makes it difficult to train a classification algorithm. Subsampling the original signal can reduce the size of the signal, but also goes along with a loss of information since details of the signal are dismissed [76]. In addition, for high-frequency signals even subsampling might not reduce the dimensionality to a tractable size. To cope with these constraints, research in the time series domain has come up with various solution. The most important ones will be presented in the following paragraphs.

In [177] a feature extraction method is defined that transforms a time series into a feature vector by extracting different statistical features like the mean

$$\mu_{\mathbf{o}_{n:m}} = \frac{\sum_{i=n}^m o_i}{m-n+1} \ , \tag{2.13}$$

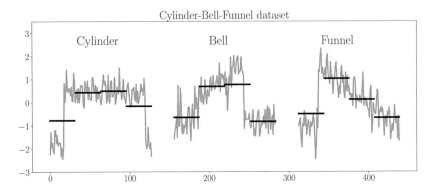

Figure 2.4: Example of instances of the classical time series classification dataset: Cylinder, Bell, Funnel provided by [214]. Here the dimensionality of the time signal is reduced by replacing parts of the signal by their mean values (PAA) [127] which are shown as black segments.

standard deviation

$$\sigma_{\mathbf{o}_{n:m}} = \frac{\sqrt{\sum_{i=n}^{m}(o_i - \mu_{\mathbf{o}_{n:m}})^2}}{m - n} \; , \tag{2.14}$$

skewness

$$\text{skew}_{\mathbf{o}_{n:m}} = \frac{\sum_{i=n}^{m}(o_i - \mu_{\mathbf{o}_{n:m}})^3}{(m - n)\sigma_{\mathbf{o}_{n:m}}^3} \tag{2.15}$$

and kurtosis

$$\text{kurt}_{\mathbf{o}_{n:m}} = \frac{\sum_{i=n}^{m}(o_i - \mu_{\mathbf{o}_{n:m}})^4}{(m - n)\sigma_{\mathbf{o}_{n:m}}^4} - 3 \tag{2.16}$$

of the time series. In addition, second-order statistical features based on the differences between the compared series are added. The authors [248] also include time specific statistical features like trend, seasonality, periodicity or serial correlation. A list of statistical features with a detailed description can also be found in [197]. The works of [172, 171, 6, 206] utilise the Discrete Fourier Transform (DFT) to convert time series from the time into the frequency domain. A reduction of dimensionality is achieved by choosing only a subset of DFT coefficients. Similar approaches can also be found for the wavelet transform [54, 201]. An extreme example of feature extraction is provided by [79, 78] in which the authors extract over 1000 different features. Besides the already mentioned statistical features like mean or skewness, they add autocorrelations, power spectrum features, entropy, auto regressive moving average (ARMA) parameters, wavelet parameters, and many others. The feature extraction is followed by a greedy forward feature selection step in which the best features for the linear discriminant classifier are searched. This feature selection method firstly uses a single feature together with the corresponding classifier. Based on a 10-fold cross-validation, the feature with the best classification rate is kept. In the next iteration, all remaining features are then combined with the single best one. Again, the feature is selected that delivers the best classification result in combination with the selected feature from the first round. This procedure is repeated until a termination criterion is reached. Here, the authors chose to end the feature selection if the classification rate does not improve more then three percent. This proposed brute-force approach is "completely data-driven and does not require any knowledge of the dynamical mechanisms underlying the time series or how they were measured" [78] but also comes with a high computational complexity during the extraction and selection phase. However, their experimental results are comparable to state-of-the-art methods.

A different way to reduce the dimensionality of time series is to summarise parts of the series and transform them into a more compact representation. In [127], the Piecewise Aggregate Approximation (PAA) method is proposed. Hereby, a longer time series is cut into shorter segments and for each segment the mean value is calculated (see Fig. 2.4). This reduces the dimensionality to the number of segments and makes two time series easier and faster comparable. This approach is further developed in [128] where the segment length is chosen adaptively. Based on PAA, the SAX (Symbolic Aggregate approXimation) method is introduced in [150, 151]. SAX performs an additional discretisation step, in which the mean values from PAA are matched to equiprobable symbols. As [221] show, instead of taking the mean value, each segment can also be represented by the parameters of a linear or polynomial function.

Multiple classification models are build on top of the SAX representation. In [152], SAX symbols of a time series are combined into a histogram which is used as feature vector for classification. SAX-VSM [219] uses a similar approach but also transforms the Bag-of-SAX-words vector into a different feature representation by using a technique from information retrieval, called tf-idf (term frequency-inverse document frequency). In the paper of [13], a detailed review of time series classification methods is given together with an exhaustive experimental evaluation. However, their datasets for time series are "equal length, real valued and have no missing values". Three instances of the classical dataset, called the Cylinder, Bell, Funnel dataset, are shown in Fig. 2.4. Since the focus of this thesis lies on time series classification for activity recognition, some properties, e.g. time series of equal length, are not given by the nature of the problem. A more detailed explanation of the specifics in sensor-based activity recognition will be given in paragraph 2.3.

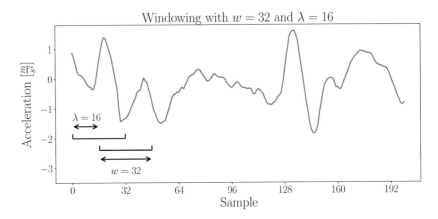

Figure 2.5: To extract features for a time series, the sequence is split into smaller subsequences of size $w = 32$. Each window is shifted by $\lambda = 16$ data points.

Segmentation   Equation (2.11) and Eq. (2.12) describe the desirable situation in Machine Learning in which each sample represents a single instance of a class. For example, for activity recognition this means that a defined period of time, e.g. five seconds, are recorded while a specific activity is performed. Despite the fact that public research datasets often provide this kind of segmentation, it rarely meets real-life use cases. Instead, the most common form to be found is a continuous stream of data.

Nevertheless, in order to be able to carry out a classification, the data stream must be divided into several smaller parts which are called *subsequences* throughout this work. This is achieved by windowing the data stream in a way that a long time series is split into several smaller time series. Thus, the series of observations $\mathbf{o}_{1:\tau}$ becomes a set of series of observations D,

$$D = \left\{ \mathbf{o}_{1:w}, \mathbf{o}_{\lambda:\lambda+w}, \mathbf{o}_{2\lambda:2\lambda+w}, \ldots, \mathbf{o}_{i:i\lambda+w}, \ldots, \mathbf{o}_{\gamma\lambda:\gamma\lambda+w} \right\}, \qquad (2.17)$$

where w is the width of the window and consequently the length of a subsequence. The parameter λ determines how many data points the window is shifted to the right (see Fig. 2.5). The total number of subsequences is given by $\gamma = \tau - w \pmod{\lambda} + 1$. Each of the short time series can now be classified separately. Almost all of the proposed classification methods that were previously described, and will be introduced later on, rely on this principle. An exception to this is shown at the end of chapter 4. However, the classification described there does not follow the standard pattern recognition approach.

Finally, a noteworthy issue occurs when more than one activity is present in a single

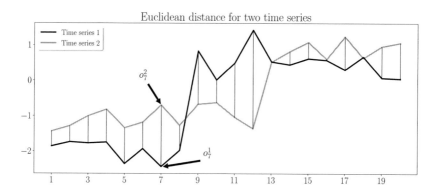

Figure 2.6: The Euclidean distance for two time series is shown as vertical lines between the aligned data points.

sequence. In such cases, a common approach is to assign the label to the sequence that appears most frequently in it. Training a classifier for such situations can be particularly difficult as different classes are mixed together.

2.2.3 Distance-based classification

A very simple benchmark classification method is the k-Nearest Neighbour (k-NN) classifier with $k = 1$. Nearest Neighbour classifiers assign a class label to an unknown sample by checking the labels of the sample's k closest neighbours. Using a majority voting schema, the newly assigned label is then the most frequent label among the neighbours. To determine which samples from the training set are the nearest ones, a distance metric like Euclidean distance can be used. The same principle applies to time series classification. Given a training set, the time series with the unknown label is compared to all the training time series. When Euclidean distance is used, the distance is calculated element-wise so that for two time series $\mathbf{o}^1_{1:\tau}$ and $\mathbf{o}^2_{1:\tau}$ the Euclidean distance is given by:

$$d_{\text{euclid}} = \sqrt{(o^1_1 - o^2_1)^2 + (o^1_2 - o^2_2)^2 + \ldots + (o^1_\tau - o^2_\tau)^2} \ . \tag{2.18}$$

Dynamic Time Warping

Dynamic Time Warping (DTW) is a distance measurement to compare two sequences with each other. DTW has its origin in speech recognition [215, 112, 25], but was since then also applied in other fields like robotics [233], gesture recognition [52, 210] and medical applications [72]. The popularity of this method origins from its ability to compare time series even if they are distorted or of unequal length. While, for example, Euclidean distance does a one-to-one mapping (see Fig. 2.6) by comparing measurement points with exact the same index, DTW is able to align one measurement point to multiple points of a second sequence (see Fig. 2.7 on the left). The only prerequisite for DTW is that points of both sequences must be equidistant. This, however, can be achieved by re-sampling the signals appropriately.

DTW compares two time series $\mathbf{o}_{1:\tau_j}^j = (o_1^j, o_2^j, \ldots, o_{t_j}^j, \ldots, o_{\tau_j}^j)^T$ and $\mathbf{o}_{1:\tau_k}^k = (o_1^k, o_2^k, \ldots, o_{t_k}^k, \ldots, o_{\tau_k}^k)^T$ with each other by calculating a cost matrix $\mathbf{C} \in \mathbb{R}^{\tau_j \times \tau_k}$ in which the entry at the position (t_j, t_k) is given by a cost function $c(t_j, t_k)$. For this cost function the Euclidean distance is often chosen, so that an entry of the matrix is

$$c(t_j, t_k) = \sqrt{(o_{t_j}^j - o_{t_k}^k)^2} \ . \tag{2.19}$$

The goal now is to find a path from $\mathbf{C}(1, 1)$ to $\mathbf{C}(\tau_j, \tau_k)$ which is called a warping path

$$\mathbf{p} = (p_1, p_2, \ldots, p_l, \ldots p_L)^T \ . \tag{2.20}$$

The l-th components $p_l = (t_{j,l}, t_{k,l})$ of the warping path are the indices of the single observations $o_{t_j}^j$ and $o_{t_k}^k$ from the sequences $\mathbf{o}_{1:\tau_j}^j$ and $\mathbf{o}_{1:\tau_k}^k$. A warping path arranges pairs of measurements of two sequences such that the distance among the points is minimised.

The generation of a warping path relies certain restrictions [175]:

- The first component p_1 and the last component p_L of the warping path are defined as $p_1 = (1, 1)$ and $p_L = (\tau_j, \tau_k)$.

- The indices within each component p_l are monotonically increasing, so that $t_{j,1} \leq t_{j,2} \leq \ldots \leq t_{j,l} \leq \ldots \leq \tau_{j,L}$ and $t_{k,1} \leq t_{k,2} \leq \ldots \leq t_{k,l} \leq \ldots \leq \tau_{k,L}$.

- $p_{l+1} - p_l \in \{(1, 0), (0, 1), (1, 1)\}$ for $1 \leq l \leq L$.

The first condition is a boundary condition that defines the start and end point of the path. The second condition prohibits the path going "backwards" and the last condition restricts next possible path components p_{l+1} to ones that are in the direct neighbourhood of the current path component p_l.

An optimal warping path is the path that minimises the total costs and can be determined recursively by the following rules which are based on dynamic programming

$$p_{l-1} = \begin{cases} (1, t_k - 1) & \text{if } t_j = 1 \\ (t_j - 1, 1) & \text{if } t_k = 1 \\ \min\left(\mathbf{C}(t_j - 1, t_k - 1), \mathbf{C}(t_j - 1, t_k), \mathbf{C}(t_j, t_k - 1)\right) & \text{otherwise} \end{cases} \ . \tag{2.21}$$

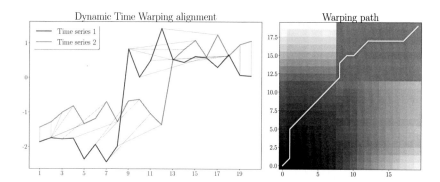

Figure 2.7: On the left side two time series are aligned by Dynamic Time Warping. Compared to the Euclidean distance in Fig. 2.6, DTW especially matches sharp peaks in the sequence much better. This is visible for the first time series at $t = 9$, that is matched with the points $t = 13, t = 14$ and $t = 15$ of the second time series. The image on the right shows the corresponding warping path. The darker the squares, the smaller the DTW. If the warping path contains only diagonal elements, DTW is equal to the Euclidean distance.

If a warping path consists only of diagonal elements, it is equivalent to the Euclidean distance measurement. The time and space complexity of DTW is $\mathcal{O}(n^2)$ if implemented recursively, but can be reduced to $\mathcal{O}(n)$ if an iterative implementation is chosen together with some optimisations [208]. An example of a warping path for the time series from Fig. 2.6 can be seen in Fig. 2.7. Additional improvements to DTW can be made by including a warping window that determines how far the warping path is allowed to deviate from the diagonal [173, 215]. Simply said, a tight window around the diagonal restricts the search for paths with optimal cost. Contrary, a window that is too large leads to an alignment of points which are far away from each other and in fact should not be connected. In addition, a tight window also decreases the computational complexity of DTW. Similar to this, [115] add a penalty to paths with high phase difference. In [84], the authors chose to use the derivative of the sequence in combination with DTW. They argue that the derivative of a signal "determines the general shape of the function rather than the value of the function at an actual point. The derivative shows what happens in the neighbourhood of the point".

One important preprocessing step is the normalisation of time sequences. The authors [173] recommend to use a z-normalisation. For this, the sequence is subtracted by its mean and divided by its standard deviation. With this, Dynamic Time Warp-

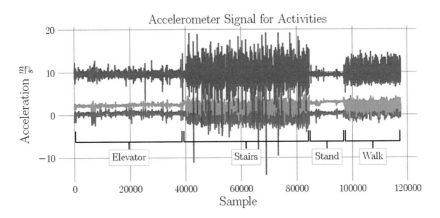

Figure 2.8: A time series that contains four different activities: riding an elevator, climbing stairs, standing and walking. The goal of time series classification is to assign to each point in time the appropriate class label.

ing was found to be a hard-to-beat competitor when combined with Nearest-Neighbour classification [13].

Finally, connecting with the previous section "Feature-based classification" (Sec. 2.2.2), DTW has recently also been used by [125] as feature for a SVM classifier. There, the features of the vector are the DTW distances to all samples from the training set. The feature vector is additionally enriched with SAX words.

2.3 Activity Recognition

The remainder of this chapter introduces the problem of sensor-based human activity recognition (HAR) as application in which time series data is used. In human activity recognition, the goal is to identify the user's current activity based on data from sensors that are attached to the body. The motivation behind this area of research rose together with the wish for context-aware computers and ambient assisted living systems as described in the introductory Chap. 1. One example of such a problem is shown in Fig. 2.8, where the accelerometer signals of typical modes of locomotion are displayed.

2.3.1 Characteristic Properties of Activity Recognition

In the review paper of [33], several challenges have been identified that apply specifically to the activity recognition problem:

- **Intraclass variability** The same activity can be performed in many different ways. For example, the activity "walking" is dependent on the walking speed, the user-specific walking style, floor material, and probably also on the shoes the user is wearing. These circumstances might cause high variations that must be covered by the classification system. One way to restrict the number of variations is to train a person-specific model. Hereby the classifier is only trained on data obtained by the user who will later also utilise the system. Contrary, user-independent systems are trained on data that not necessarily include the future user. For this, either a large amount of data is needed or features must be developed that are user-independent. It can be expected that the user-specific model delivers better results than the independent one. However, it also requires the collection of individual training data.

  A different example of intraclass variability is caused by sensor displacement. Often training data is collected with a specific sensor setup in which the sensor placement is fixed at a certain orientation and position. To avoid this effect, again the training data can be enlarged by different sensor positions or features are created that are invariant to such changes [139, 18].

- **NULL class problem** Looking at the stream of data for a typical day of a user, usually only a small portion of his activities are relevant for a HAR system. The other portion should be ignored by the system. These irrelevant parts are known as the NULL class or rejection class [181]. In consequence, a HAR system must be able to distinguish between activities it was trained on and NULL class activities. The challenge here, however, is that activities that belong to the NULL class are usually unknown to the system which makes it complicated to train the system for these cases.

- **Class imbalance** One has to take special care if one specific activity occurs disproportionately frequent compared to other activities. For example, given a typical office worker and the activities walking, sitting and climbing stairs, the amount of sitting-time will probably dominate his day, followed by walking and climbing stairs. This becomes a problem, if some classes occur so rarely that the amount of training data is not sufficient to train the system. Additionally, it is important to choose the correct metric when evaluating the classifier. For imbalanced class setups, the authors [39] recommend to use the weighted F1-

measure

$$F_1 = \sum_i 2w_i \frac{\text{precision}_i \cdot \text{recall}_i}{\text{precision}_i + \text{recall}_i} \tag{2.22}$$

with

$$\text{precision} = \frac{\text{TP}}{\text{TP} + \text{FP}} \tag{2.23}$$

and

$$\text{recall} = \frac{\text{TP}}{\text{TP} + \text{FN}} \ . \tag{2.24}$$

Here, i represents the index of the class, $w_i = \frac{n_i}{N}$ is the ratio between the number of samples of the i-th class n_i and the total number of samples N. TP, TN, FP and FN are the number of true positives, true negatives, false positives and false negatives.

- **Data collection** Collecting data is a special challenge in activity recognition. In HAR usually many sensors are used that are distributed around the user's body. For example, the Opportunity dataset contains measurements from 15 sensors [39]. In such a case, special care must be given to the synchronisation of all measurement devices [34]. Also, since most data is not processed on the measurement device itself, but on a central computer, there is always the danger that some data gets lost due to connection issues.

- **Data annotation** As described, supervised learning methods require labelled data so that collected data also needs to be annotated. In activity recognition this annotation is difficult because i) in contrast to e.g. object recognition in images, it is very hard to identify an activity by simply looking at the sequence of recorded sensor data. Thus, labels must be assigned to the data already during the recording. This can be done by either the user himself or by an external observer. Self-reporting by the user entails the risk that annotations are inaccurate or even wrong. Annotation by an external observer, however, is labour-intensive and time-consuming. Additionally, such a setup almost always requires laboratory conditions which is known to influence participants' behaviour in an unnatural way. ii) it is hard to define the point of time when an activity starts and when it ends. This is even true for the most simple activities like drinking. Does the activity start when the user grabs the cup or when he takes the first sip? Does it end when the user puts the cup back on the table or after finishing to swallow? Since there is no agreed-on definition for any of these activities, this might lead to confusion when labelling data.

- **Overlapping activities** Often activities are performed at the same time. This becomes an issue for the HAR system if these activities influence measurements of the same device. Again, using the example of walking and drinking, the data for "drinking" and "drinking during walking" will look dissimilar. Nevertheless, training a HAR on all possible combinations of activities is out of scope.

- **Measurability of activities** Some activities might not be recognisable because the effect of the activity is not measured by any sensor. Obviously, detecting a drinking activity is not possible if the sensor is in the trouser pocket of the user.

2.3.2 Examples of Activity Recognition

In the next paragraphs, examples for activity classification will be illustrated. The first one shows how the fusion of different sensor data can be used to determine the locomotion mode of persons. Afterwards, details will be given about how step recognition can be carried out. This serves as a preliminary work for the models in the field of indoor localisation in Chap. 4. The chapter concludes with an example from the field of emotion recognition where stress is recognised based on physiological data.

Recognition of Motion Activities

The aim in the following is to classify people's different ways of locomotion. These include walking, standing, climbing or descending stairs and taking the elevator up or down. As described in Sec. 2.2.2, the streaming sensor data is split in multiple subsequences. Each subsequence is then represented as a set of features.

In this case, the classification is only carried out using the sensors of the smartphone. In particular, it can be shown that the acceleration signal and the barometer are sufficient for this task. Hereby, the acceleration signal is used to detect the movement of the person by calculating the magnitude of the variance of each accelerometer axis with

$$\text{mag}_{\text{acc}} = \sqrt{\sigma_{\text{acc},x}^2 + \sigma_{\text{acc},y}^2 + \sigma_{\text{acc},z}^2} \ . \tag{2.25}$$

Motion activities are characterised by a higher variance in the time signal than nonmovements. In Fig. 2.9 this is visible in the three most-right clusters that represent the classes walking and climbing stairs up and down. Hence, with this it is already possible to group activities into motion and standing activities. A change in altitude can now be detected by means of the barometer. For this, the difference between the last and the first barometer value is picked as distinguishing feature since it depicts changes of the barometer value during a given period of time. Based on this information, activities that cause a height difference can be distinguished.

Combining all these different separations results in four activity quadrants as seen in Fig. 2.9. Thereby, everything left of the vertical dashed line denotes activities without

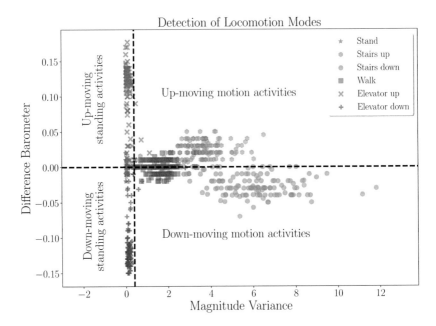

Figure 2.9: Based on the two features "Barometer difference" and "Magnitude Variance", the six locomotion classes can already be separated visibly. The vertical dashed line denotes the separation between activities that include motion, like walking and climbing stairs, and non-motion activities, like standing and using the elevator. The horizontal dashed line distinguishes between up-moving and down-moving activities.

active motion, while classes to the right include motion. Activities that cause altitude changes, appear on opposite sides of the horizontal boarder. Already in this graph it is visible that the stair-related activities have a higher variance, but can be distinguished among each other due to the barometer change. Walking has a somewhat lower variance and also no differences in the barometer values. Both cases of the usage of the elevator can be separated by the barometer values alone. And just standing results in almost all values to be close to zero. Based on these two features, classifiers like Naives Bayes or a Decision Tree can be successfully trained.

Step detection Estimating a step from the sensors of the IMU is a long-standing problem for which many solutions are possible [162]. Looking at the accelerometer

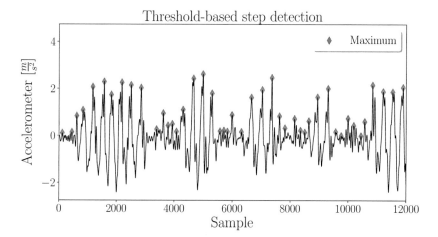

Figure 2.10: A common way to detect steps is to find the maximum value in the accelerometer signal and compare it to a previously learned threshold.

signal a repetitive pattern is visible that can be exploited. Since the impact of the foot produces a strong amplitude in the accelerometer signal, one of the most popular methods for the detection of steps is to find peaks in the signal that are above a certain threshold [123, 43, 227, 147, 153]. As proposed by the author of this thesis in [70, 66], a threshold-based step detection should also be complemented by a short period of time, e.g. 300 ms, in which no other step can be detected to reduce the false positive rate.

The main problem with this approach is that the threshold often is person-dependent, dependent on the surface and the walking speed. To avoid manual adjustment of this threshold, it is typically learned from a set of training data [180].

Besides the usage of thresholds, also different features like Fourier coefficients, wavelets and autocorrelation have been used for step detection [20, 207] since they capture the repetitive nature of the signal. Furthermore, often not only the pure detection of steps is needed, but also an estimation of the corresponding step length is of interest. One trivial approach is to estimate a fixed stride length which however works surprisingly well for many applications. Other solutions rely on the step frequency [147, 260] or take the vertical acceleration into account [252].

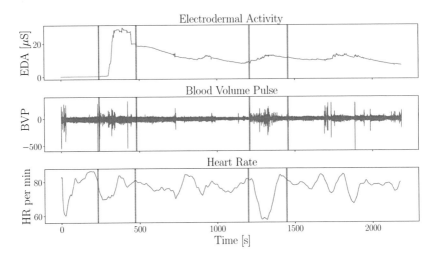

Figure 2.11: Example of a stress test that was conducted on a single person. The area marked by the red bars highlight the period when the subject had to dip his hands in ice cold water. For all three sensors increasing values are visible. Similarly, the area marked by the green bars shows an instance of a Stroop test taken by the subject. While the electrodermal activity and the blood volume pulse show an increasing activity, the heart rate drops significantly. There is no clear reasoning for this observation, but one cannot exclude a malfunction of the sensor. However, such examples show that the collection and interpretation of the activity recognition data often is a challenging task.

Example of Emotion Recognition

Many sensors that were initially designed for medical purposes are now also available in commercial wearable devices (see Chap. 1). These include, in particular, sensors for measuring heart rate (HR), electrical conductivity of the skin and body temperature [80]. Based on these physiological signals, attempts to recognize emotional stress in daily life with the goal of health prevention [16] or intelligent human-machine interactions [198] have been researched. Emotional stress can be roughly divided into three groups: acute, episodic and chronic stress [22]. Acute stress happens on a daily basis and is caused by short events, but is generally not harmful as long as its frequency does not increase over a longer period. However, if stress situations occur over a long period of time, they can result in significant negative effects on the person's health.

Most research work focuses on the detection of acute stress situations based on

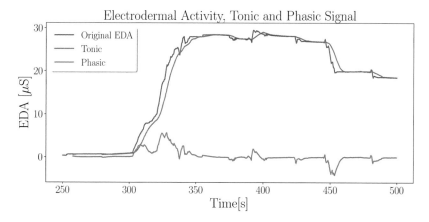

Figure 2.12: The electrodermal activity signal can be decomposed into a tonic and a phasic component. The tonic signal represents a long-term base level and is calculated as the rolling mean of the original EDA signal. The phasic signal is the difference between the original EDA and the tonic signal and is used to identify short and rapid signal changes.

electrodermal activity and heart rate information. For the latter, often typical statistical features like the mean, variance, amplitude, number of peaks, and Fourier coefficients are calculated [85] as features.

In order to calculate features for the EDA sensor, the signal is split into a tonic and a phasic part as shown in Fig. 2.12. The tonic skin conductance level is an average value to identify longer term changes and to establish a baseline level for a specific person. Contrary, the phasic skin conductance response is used to identify rapidly changing peaks and short term events [90]. Based on the tonic and phasic signals various works have tried to identify stress events using the methods introduced in Chap. 2.2 [85, 91, 16, 90]. It is important to include information from other sensors when using the EDA sensor since sweating can also be caused by external influences, e.g. because the person is currently exercising or sweating due to the warm weather. In order to exclude such cases, one can use the previously mentioned methods to detect physical activities.

In order to make stress measurable under laboratory conditions, various test scenarios have been developed in the past. For this, artificial stress generators are used, e.g. immersion of the hands in ice-cold water, calculation of mathematical problems under a time limitation and Stroop tests. Stroop tests are used to identify the reaction of subjects to contradicting inputs and unfamiliar situations. An example of such is to show persons colour words like "red", "green" or "blue" on a screen, however the words are written in a different colour than they represent. The test person has to name the colour in which the word is written as fast as possible.

One instance of such a stress test, where the electrodermal activity, the heart rate and the blood volume pulse are measured, is shown in Fig. 2.11. Hereby, different stress tests are carried out with small resting phases in-between. The blood volume pulse (BVP) indicates the variation of volume of arterial blood under the skin [80] .

Chapter 3

A General Framework for Human Activity Recognition

The following chapter introduces a framework for human activity recognition. The main motivation behind this framework is the elderly care sector with the aim of enabling older people to live longer in their own homes instead of moving into a retirement home [1]. Given this scenario, two main considerations should be taken into account. People want to retain sovereignty over their private sphere and, for example, be able to specifically switch off sensors that they find unpleasant in certain situations. On the other hand, a solution should be cost-effective. This is achieved primarily by using inexpensive sensors and computing hardware. The proposed framework therefore will only use the previously introduced sensors from wearable devices. For the activity recognition part of this framework a method is proposed that extracts features from underlying sensor data without manual intervention and domain knowledge. This so-called feature learning approach is based on the generation of a codebook and the transformation of raw signals into codewords. Within this method, sensor data are fused in such a way that a user of the system can switch sensors on an off on demand. In contrast to existing feature learning methods from the deep learning area, only a small number of hyper-parameters are used within the proposed approach. Since the activity recognition takes place on a central server, the data has to be transferred from the wearable devices to the server. For this, the open message-based protocol AMQP (Advanced Message Queuing Protocol) is used.

3.1   Related Work

What follows is a brief overview of other solutions in the field of smart home sensor technology. Subsequently, an outline is given about research in the sector of feature learning.

3.1.1   Smart Home Technology

Smart home technologies and activity recognition are traditionally overlapping research areas. Smart homes are characterised by an active monitoring of their residents' context by trying to grasp the current activity and support them appropriately by delivering information or actions required at that time. Often such solutions rely on cameras and microphones. However, these sensors raise issues regarding the user's privacy and are therefore not always suitable.

One way to use simple and cheap sensor technology is to utilise motion sensors. These are mounted in different places in the house or are attached to articles of daily use like microwaves or toilets. The outputs of such sensors are binary values indicating the presence of a person in a specific location or the usage of an item [237, 158, 196, 94].

One popular example is the living lab "PlaceLab" [109] which is an apartment of approximately 1000 sq. ft. equipped with various different sensors and computational hardware. The available sensors include cameras and microphones, but for many experiments participants were asked to also wear accelerometers and gyroscopes. Sensor data are transferred to and synchronised at a central server. In the work of [158] this laboratory was used to observe the daily behaviour of a married couple over a timespan of ten weeks. By comparing the activity recognition results across different sensor modalities, [158] have shown that for most activities the location of the user is a strong indicator for his/her current activity. Similar, the Gator Tec Smart House [102] was also equipped with a wide variety of sensors. However, the researchers have also put a strong focus on the software architecture that should allow an effortless integration of new sensors. For this purpose, developers can access the raw sensor data over an abstraction layer without the need to understand how the data was generated. The CASAS system developed by [51] is a pre-packed tool box that is designed to be especially user-friendly. In this system mainly motion sensors are used that the user can install on his own. Additionally, the system is designed to be easily extendible by additional sensors. The authors emphasise the low cost of this solution since only a small server is needed to perform activity recognition. The costs for the complete system are about $2765 at the time of their publication.

3.1.2 Feature Learning

In Chap. 2 methods for time series classification were introduced. One commonality of these methods was that features had to be extracted manually from the underlying data. This usually requires substantial domain knowledge and a good understanding of the process of how the underlying data was generated. A good selection of features covers several important aspects. Firstly, features are a compact representation of the underlying data which reduces the computational complexity for later processing steps. Secondly, a reduced representation of data helps to avoid the "curse of dimensionality" [63] since less training samples are required to cover a small-dimensional feature space. Thirdly, features should contain the information that is relevant for the final classification [181]. In consequence, feature vectors that belong to the same class should form a compact and disjoint region in the feature space [114]. For example, a useful feature to distinguish between images of "apples" and of "bananas" could be the dominant colour in the image (e.g. red for apples in comparison to yellow for bananas).

However, the question of "how to extract good features" is still open. Niemann [181] lists two general approaches for feature extraction. The first one is based on domain knowledge and empirical testing. The designer of the pattern recognition system has to use its intuition and experience to find valuable features. The second approach is based on analytical methods which are extracting "optimal" features in regard to a predefined optimisation criterion. Here, methods like the Principal Component Analysis (PCA) exist that transform a pattern into a lower-dimensional feature space. Still, often enough the search for features ends up in a trial-and-error approach until a sufficient set of features was found. Time series classification is in particular a difficult task for manual feature extraction, since it is hard for humans to find important characteristics by just looking at the time series. This is especially the case when many signals are recorded simultaneously.

Counting the frequency of relevant pieces of information in the data has gained a lot of attention due to both its simplicity and effectiveness. In image recognition this principle is known as Bag-of-visual words [53, 117]. A large number of small regions is extracted from images and used to learn characteristic properties by grouping these regions using for example K-means clustering [50] (see Fig. 3.1). The extracted and clustered sub-images form the so-called codewords of a larger codebook. Thus, each image is represented by the distribution of codewords that can be found in it. This principle can also be applied to time series classification as shown in areas like activity and emotion recognition [21, 222]. In [246, 247] a codebook-based method is used to extract information from biomedical time series. The extracted histograms of codewords are compared distance-wise with a Nearest Neighbour approach. Similar, in [187] SAX words are extracted and used for a Bag-of-Patterns approach.

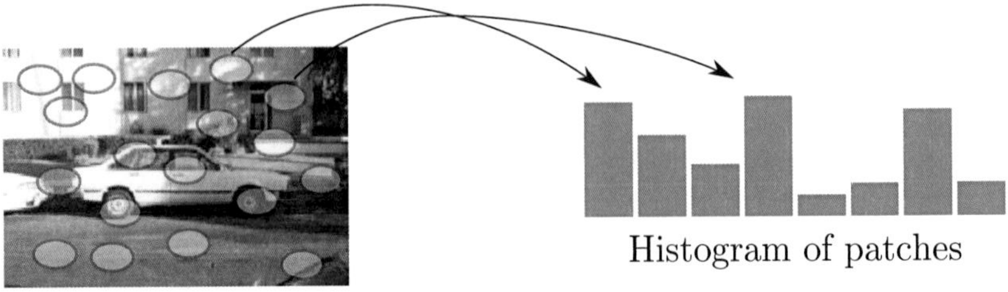

Histogram of patches

Figure 3.1: A well-known technique in image recognition is to extract various small sub-images (patches) from the main image. An image is then represented by the frequency of characteristic patches.

In the last years research in the Machine Learning field has focused more intensively on *feature learning* approaches, also known as *representation learning*. The basic idea behind feature learning is to replace the manual feature extraction step by a methodology that can be applied independently from the task and domain. As stated by [23], such a representation would make Machine Learning "less dependent on feature engineering so that novel applications could be constructed faster, and more importantly, to make progress toward artificial intelligence (AI)." Thus, in the presented problem of activity recognition in time series classification it should not matter if the task is to recognise locomotion based on accelerometer data or emotional stress based on the data of electrodermal measurements of skin.

Typically, feature learning is associated with the term of deep learning, where neural networks with multiple hidden layers are used. For example, autoencoders and convolutional neural networks are applied by [200, 163, 170] to extract feature representations. In [205] a Restricted Boltzman Machine is applied to a multimodal dataset. To capture temporal dependencies, [95] use a recurrent neural network for feature extraction and classification. Despite the success of deep learning methods, one major disadvantage is the large number of hyper-parameters that require to be optimised. Among these parameters are the learning rate, the learning rate schedule, the mini-batch size, the number of training iterations, the number of hidden units, the weight decay and the initial weights [24].

Due to this fact, a codebook approach is proposed in this work that only uses a small number of intuitive parameters, namely the size of the sliding window, the amount of samples this window is shifted and the number of codewords. Based on this method a general framework for activity recognition is introduced that is applicable to sensor types that produce time series data. The author has contributed to this work in the publications that can be found in [222, 136].

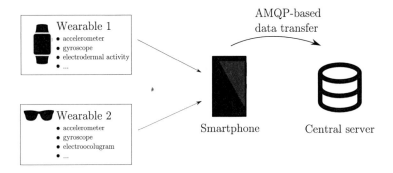

Figure 3.2: An overview of an implementation of the activity recognition framework. A smartwatch and smartglasses are connected to a smartphone to which they send their data. The phone sends the collected data to the central server where the final activity recognition takes place.

3.2 System Architecture Overview

In this section a description for a genefal framework for activity recognition is provided. The framework can be divided into three parts (see Fig. 3.2). The first part deals with the data acquisition by utilising sensors from wearable devices. This includes, but is not restricted to sensors, like accelerometers, gyroscopes and magnetometers from devices like smartphones, smartwaches and smartglasses. The second component takes over the task of data transfer. In particular, the data has to be sent from the smartphone to a central server component. Finally, the central server depicts the last component of the framework. The central server receives the collected sensor data and applies the proposed codebook-based activity recognition method. The results of the activity recognition algorithm can be sent back to the user's smartphone or stored for later use.

3.2.1 Data Acquisition

The framework is designed in a way that multiple different devices can connect to it while each device can have one or more different types of sensors included. The only requirement is that the output of a sensor is a time series which fits to all of the sensors that were described in this thesis.

However, during the data collection some properties are important to be aware of. Firstly, the sampling frequency with which sensors collect data could potentially influence the accuracy of an activity recognition system. This is especially the case if very short activities should be recognised. For current wearable devices the typical recording frequency lies in the area of 20Hz up to 200Hz. Though, the framework does not impose any conditions on the sampling frequency. Secondly, the position of the sensor can impact the performance of the recognition system as explored in [137, 19, 10, 49]. For example, a sensor might be tightened upside down. This phenomenon can be encountered by either collecting training data that includes various sensor positions, or by using position-invariant features. Finally, many activities can only be recognised if an appropriate sensor is attached to a specific body part. For example, activities that include arm movement can naturally only be measured by an arm-attached sensor. As will be shown throughout this chapter and in the experimental results, the combination of multiple sensors will lead to the best overall results. The proposed framework offers the possibility to fuse different kinds of sensors.

3.2.2   Data Transfer

Although most mobile devices have sufficient computational resources to process the data on the device itself, this is usually at the expense of a higher battery consumption. Hence, all data is send to a central server where the data is collected and activity recognition is performed. In this thesis the Advanced Message Queuing Protocol (AMQP) is used [239] as an exemplary data transfer method, but could be exchanged by any other appropriate transfer protocol. AMQP transfers data in form of messages and takes especially care of putting data into a queue or resending it if the data receiver cannot be reached. However, since the data transfer is not in the focus of this work, only a short summary of the method will be given.

A first data transfer takes place in the transmission of the data from the smartwach and smartglasses to the smartphone. This is needed since most wearable devices are directly linked with the smartphone and do not offer the possibility to transfer their data directly to a central server. This data transfer is typically handled with a Low Energy Bluetooth connection. With ever more powerful wearable devices this step might become obsolete in the near future, allowing the data to be directly sent to the server instead of taking the detour via the smartphone. In the presented solution, however, the smartphone represents a temporal data storage.

In the next step, the data must be transferred from the phone to the central server using the AMQP protocol. For this, RabbitMQ [203] as popular implementation of AMPQ is used. Using this implementation on the phone results in a middleware that receives and routes messages from the data producers to the appropriate data receivers. Hereby, each sensor takes the role of a data producer, while components that are analysing the data act as receivers, e.g. the activity recognition algorithms. Assuming different specialised recognition models for multiple recognition tasks, e.g. model A that recognises motion activities, while model B recognises emotional activities. In such a setup, model A might need data from the accelerometer, but probably not from the heart-rate sensor. Contrary, model B might rely on data from electrodermal activity measurements, but not from gyroscope data. Using the AMQP protocol, the transfer layer can be configured in such a way that it forwards the required data to the appropriate receivers. Also, as soon as a new sensor becomes available to the system, for example a sensor to measure a person's respiration rate as additional information for the emotion recognition, the component only needs to register itself as new receiver of the data. Since the connection between the server and the smartphone can be used bidirectional, the final recognition results can be sent back to the user.

3.3 Codebook-based Feature Learning

In the following, a method is presented that extracts features without the need to include domain knowledge and that only requires a small number of parameters. The proposed method can be decomposed into three parts. Firstly, a codebook is learned from an unlabelled dataset. Secondly, to represent sequences from the underlying time series as a feature vector, each sequence is encoded as a set of codebook entries. Thirdly, a classifier is trained on the basis of the extracted feature representation.

In this work a dataset is defined as a longer period of measurements from multiple sensors, for example the sensor measurements of a wearable device over a timespan of 24 hours for a single person. Such a dataset will probably contain multiple class labels, e.g. activities like walking, running, sitting and sleeping. A dataset will be broken down into smaller parts which are called sequences of size w_{seq}. Following the introduced notation from Chap. 2.2.1, the sequence from sensors s is denoted as $\mathbf{o}^s_{1:\tau_s}$. The goal is to assign a class label y to each sequence. In the proposed approach each sequence is itself subdivided again into smaller subsequences $\mathbf{o}^s_{n:m}$ of size w_{sub}. This principle is shown in Fig. 3.3.

3.3.1 Codebook Construction

The below described procedure is performed for each sensor s: Given an unlabelled dataset, subsequences $\mathbf{o}^s_{n:m}$ of equal length w^s_{sub} are extracted from this dataset with a shifting size of λ^s_{sub} as described in Chap. 2.2.2 and shown exemplary for three subsequences in Fig. 3.4.

The extracted subsequences are grouped into N^s_ψ different clusters. Each cluster centre represents a codeword ψ^s_i and the set of all codewords builds the codebook Ψ^s,

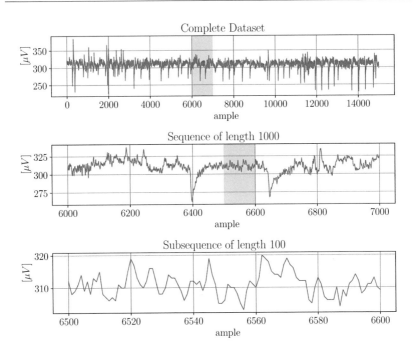

Figure 3.3: From top to bottom: A dataset is split into smaller sequences while the sequence itself is again decomposed into subsequences. The goal is to assign a class label to each sequence. Subsequences are transformed into codewords and used as feature representation.

so that

$$\Psi^s = \left\{ \psi_1^s, \psi_2^s, \ldots, \psi_{N_\psi}^s \right\} \ . \tag{3.1}$$

The number N_ψ^s denotes the number of codewords that should be used. Since the optimum number of codewords varies from case to case, the best parameter setting must be determined experimentally. The same applies to the parameters w_{sub}^s and λ_{sub}^s which specify the length and the density with which subsequences are extracted from the underlying dataset. However, it has already been shown in previous studies in image recognition that a dense extraction of subsequences often is preferable compared to a narrow extraction [182, 224].

As clustering algorithm K-means is used with the Euclidean distance as distance measurement between the subsequences. K-means is an unsupervised learning method

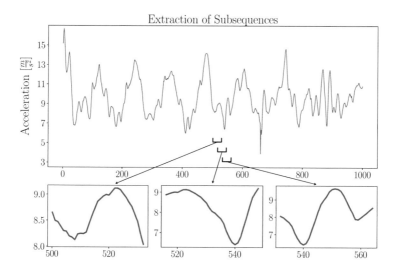

Figure 3.4: Subsequences are extracted from an unlabelled dataset. These subsequences will be used to generate a codebook.

that is based on the Expectation Maximisation (EM) algorithm and optimises the objective function

$$J = \sum_{n=1}^{N} \sum_{k=1}^{K} r_{nk} \|\mathbf{x}_n - \boldsymbol{\mu}_k\| \ , \tag{3.2}$$

where $r_{nk} \in \{0, 1\}, k = 0, \dots K$ is an indicator variable that describes to which of the K clusters a data point $\mathbf{x}_n$ is assigned to and $\boldsymbol{\mu}_k$ is a cluster centre [27]. Here, the data point $\mathbf{x}_n$ represents the subsequence $\mathbf{o}_{n:m}^s$. To find appropriate values for r_{nk} and $\boldsymbol{\mu}_k$, two steps are repeated iteratively. In a first step the centre of each cluster centre is updated by taking the mean value of the subsequences belonging to the specific cluster. In a second step, each subsequence is assigned to the cluster with the smallest distance to the cluster centre. These two steps are iterated until the cluster centres converge (see Fig. 3.5). Finally, since K-means clustering chooses cluster centres randomly during the initialisation, it is conducted multiple times until convergence. The result that yields the minimum sum of Euclidean distances between subsequences and their corresponding cluster centres is chosen as the best one and the cluster centres form the codewords. The extraction of subsequences and their clustering is done separately for each sensor, so that it ends up with s different codebooks.

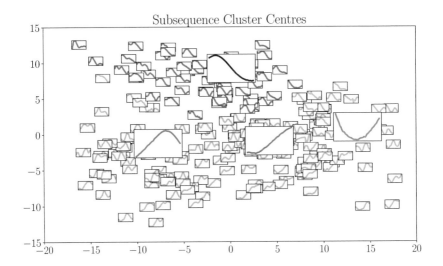

Figure 3.5: Example of K-means clustering for subsequences. The centre of each cluster will be used as a codeword within the codebook and is shown enlarged. In this example overall 2844 subsequences were clustered into four clusters. For the sake of clarity for each cluster centre only 60 subsequences were plotted.

3.3.2 Feature Representation

In the previous step a codebook was built for each single sensor. This codebook will be used in the following step to construct a feature vector for a sequence $\mathbf{o}_{1:\tau}$ that can be used to train a classifier.

The sequence $\mathbf{o}_{1:\tau}$ is split into multiple subsequences $\mathbf{o}_{n:m}$ of size w_{sub} using a sliding window that is shifted λ time indices, following the same procedure like in the codebook construction step. Each subsequence is then assigned to the most similar codeword $\widehat{\psi}$, whereby similarity is measured by a distance function $d(\cdot)$, e.g. Euclidean distance, so that

$$\widehat{\psi} = \arg\min_{\psi_i} d(\psi_i, \mathbf{o}_{n:m}) \ . \tag{3.3}$$

A sequence is therefore characterized by the distribution of codewords it contains. More precisely, each sequence represents a histogram of all N_ψ codewords. As a last step, the histogram is normalised so that the codeword frequencies sum to one. The frequency

$F(\psi_i)$ for the i-th codeword is then given by

$$F(\psi_i) = \frac{1}{N_\psi} \sum_{i}^{N_\psi} I_\psi(\psi_i) \ , \tag{3.4}$$

where $I_\psi(\psi_i)$ is an indicator function

$$I_\psi(\psi_i) = \begin{cases} 1, & \text{if codeword } \psi_i \text{ occurs in sequence} \\ 0, & \text{else} \end{cases} . \tag{3.5}$$

The assignment of a subsequence to one specific codeword is also called "hard assignment" since it deterministically maps a subsequence to a single codeword. However, often subsequences are similar to multiple codewords. For example, in Fig. 3.5 multiple instances of subsequences can be found that could belong to either of two cluster centres. This is especially true when looking at subsequences at the boarder of two clusters where the similarity between such subsequences is high, but the distances to their corresponding cluster centres are large. In this case, "soft assignment" can be used which is a way to assign subsequences to multiple codewords at once [235].

Let $\mathbf{o}_{n:m}^{(j)}$ be the j-th subsequence of a total of γ subsequences in a given sequence and ψ_i be the i-th codeword of a total of N_ψ codewords, respectively. A smoothed frequency $F(\psi_i)$ of the codeword ψ_i is given by:

$$F(\psi_i) = \frac{1}{\gamma} \sum_{j=1}^{\gamma} \frac{K_\sigma(d(\mathbf{o}_{n:m}^{(j)}, \psi_i))}{\sum_{i'=1}^{N_\psi} K_\sigma(d(\mathbf{o}_{n:m}^{(j)}, \psi_{i'}))}, \tag{3.6}$$

where

$$K_\sigma(d(\mathbf{o}_{n:m}^{(j)}, \psi_i)) = \frac{1}{\sqrt{2\pi}\sigma} \exp\left(-\frac{d(\mathbf{o}_{n:m}^{(j)}, \psi_i)^2}{2\sigma^2}\right) . \tag{3.7}$$

Here, the Euclidean distance between a subsequence and a codeword is given by $d(\mathbf{o}_{n:m}^{(j)}, \psi_i)$ while $K_\sigma(d(\mathbf{o}_{n:m}^{(j)}, \psi_i))$ represents the Gaussian kernel value with smoothness parameter σ. As usual for Gaussian functions, large σ values indicate a high standard deviation and cause frequencies of all codewords to become similar. Hence, when the distance between a subsequence and a codeword is small, $K_\sigma(d(\mathbf{o}_{n:m}^{(j)}, \psi_i))$ becomes large and consequently the subsequence $\mathbf{o}_{n:m}^{(j)}$ has a high contribution to the the frequency $F(\psi_i)$. The contribution of each subsequence is normalised by the sum of kernel values across all codewords, given in the denominator of Eq. (3.6). Using soft assignment, the final histogram represents a smoothed distribution of the codewords based on their similarities to all subsequences.

To avoid numerical underflow when computing the contribution of $\mathbf{o}_{n:m}^{(j)}$ in regard to $F(\psi_i)$, the fraction within the sum in Eq. (3.6) can be rewritten using the log-function

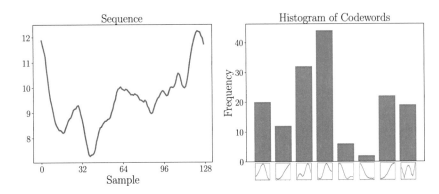

Figure 3.6: The sequence on the left is transformed into a feature representation that is given by a histogram of codewords that appear in the sequence.

[176]

$$\log \frac{K_\sigma(d(\mathbf{o}_{n:m}^{(j)}, \psi_i))}{\sum_{i'=1}^{N_\psi} K_\sigma(d(\mathbf{o}_{n:m}^{(j)}, \psi_{i'}))}$$

$$= \log K_\sigma(d(\mathbf{o}_{n:m}^{(j)}, \psi_i)) - \log \sum_{i'}^{N_\psi} \exp\left(\log K_\sigma(d(\mathbf{o}_{n:m}^{(j)}, \psi_{i'}))\right) \tag{3.8}$$

$$= -\frac{d(\mathbf{o}_{n:m}^{(j)}, \psi_i)^2}{2\sigma^2} - \sum_{i'}^{N_\psi} \exp -\frac{d(\mathbf{o}_{n:m}^{(j)}, \psi_{i'})}{2\sigma^2} \ . \tag{3.9}$$

By using the log-sum-exp trick, the sum in Eq. (3.9) is calculated by the exponentials of differences between subsequences and codewords. With this, the problem of numerical underflow can be bypassed. As can be seen, while the soft assignment strategy allows a smoother mapping of subsequence to codewords, it also comes with additional computation costs.

Summarising, the feature vector $\mathbf{c}$ is given by the normalised counts of codewords given in the specific sequence.

3.3.3 Classifier Training

Finally, a classifier is trained and tested based on the previously extracted feature representation. As outlined in Fig. 3.7 each sequence can be considered as a point in a multi-dimensional feature space. A classifier draws a classification boundary in this multi-dimensional space between sequences from different activity classes. To learn such a decision boundary the classifier is shown various examples from a labelled training dataset.

The focus here lies on the binary classifier that distinguishes between two classes, where one class is called "positive sequences" while the second class is called "negative sequences". To enable the classifier to distinguish classes of different activities from each other, hundreds of codewords are needed. However, the large number of codewords also leads to a high-dimensional feature space. Support Vector Machines (SVM) have proven to be an appropriate classification algorithm for such cases due to their effectiveness for high-dimensional data [238]. SVMs are based on the principle of "margin maximisation". A decision boundary between two classes is learned in such a way that the distance between positive and negative sequences is maximised. With this, the generalisation error becomes independent of the number of dimensions [238]. Based on the distance of a sequence from the decision boundary, the SVM outputs a score between 0 and 1 as the result of a classification [37]. In order to be able to use the binary classifier also for the multi-class case, in total κ SVMs are trained for a number of κ classes. Each of these classifiers is in itself a binary classifier. A sequence is then assigned to the class with the highest SVM score. The combination of a codebook-based feature generation with thousands of features and the classification with SVMs has been already successfully applied in image and video recognition [117].

As described in Sec. 2.3.1 one characteristic of activity recognition is the imbalanced class problem. Negative sequences significantly outweigh the number of positive sequences, since they can occur in all possible variations [99]. Due to this variability, it can happen that a classifier emphasises features on which it can classify negative sequences with high accuracy. These features, however, might be meaningless for the class of positive sequences. In the work of [223] it has been experimentally shown that SVM classifiers are not influenced by the imbalanced class problem, even if the ratio between negative and positive sequences is exceeded by 200:1. In order to accomplish a general framework without the effort of setting up too many parameters, the SVM is used with a Radial Basis Function (RBF) kernel that only requires a single parameter γ to control the complexity of the decision boundary. A general way to set this parameter is to use the mean of squared Euclidean distances among training sequences [264]. In addition, the C parameter that controls the mis-classification penalty is set to 2. Such a setting has been proven to be work for different activity recognition applications [222].

3.3.4 Fusion of Multiple Features

Since multiple sensors are used to gather different characteristics of an activity, a mechanism is needed to fuse extracted features of those sensors. In addition, a special focus is

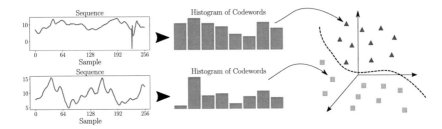

Figure 3.7: Each histogram of codewords becomes a point in a multi-dimensional feature space. Based on examples provided in a training phase, the classifier learns a decision boundary that separates different classes from each other.

put on the ability to dynamically switch sensors on and off while the recognition system is in use.

Here, three different fusing approaches are described that are also depicted in Fig. 3.8.

- **Early Fusion** In the early fusion approach for each of the M individual sensors an own codebook of length N_ψ is generated. Consequently, every sensor output is encoded as a histogram-type feature. These feature vectors are concatenated into one common feature of length MN_ψ on which basis a single SVM is trained [226]. Removing or adding a new sensor requires a re-training of the SVM for the specific combination of sensors. Hence, if the system should be able to dynamically add or remove sensors, SVMs on all possible combinations of feature vectors have to be trained.

- **Late Fusion** Contrary to the early fusion, in the late fusion approach a separate SVM is trained for each sensor based on the sensor-specific codebook outputs. Given a multi-modal sequence $\mathbf{O}_{1:\tau}$ that should be classified, its SVM score $f(\mathbf{O}_{1:\tau})$ is obtained by a linear combination of the M different SVMs as

$$f(\mathbf{O}_{1:\tau}) = \sum_{s=1}^{M} w_s f_s(\mathbf{o}_{1:\tau_s}), \ \sum_{s=1}^{M} w_s = 1, \ w_s \geq 0 \ . \tag{3.10}$$

To compute the weights w_s, the original training dataset is split into two equally-sized subsets [226]. The first subset is used to train a SVM for each of the different sensors, while the second one is used as testing dataset. The purpose of this testing set is to find weights w_s that optimise the recognition performance for this subset. As optimisation method gradient descent is applied. The optimised weights are then utilised for the complete training set. One key assumption that is made by

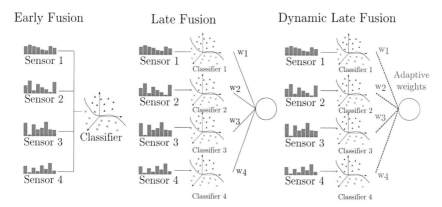

Figure 3.8: On the left side the early fusion approach is illustrated, where one common feature vector of all sensors is used to train a classifier. The late fusion approach in the middle weights every sensor to achieve an optimal result. The dynamic late fusion approach on the right side uses computed weights based on the combination of all possible sensors. Whenever a sensor is turned off, the particular weight is set to zero and the remaining weights are normalised.

this approach is that the weights that were optimised on a subset of the training dataset can again be used for SVMs that are trained on the complete training dataset. In particular, this assumption will be satisfied if the training data can be split into similar subsets. It would also be conceivable to carry out a cross-validation with different splits into subsets and average the optimised weights. However, the computational effort would significantly increase with such an approach. Similar to the early fusion approach, for all different combinations of sensors the appropriate weights and classifiers have to be calculated if a dynamic sensor selection component should be included in the system.

- **Dynamic Late Fusion** To overcome the expensive computational costs for re-training SVMs for all possible combinations of sensors in the early and late fusion approach, a simpler dynamic fusion approach can also be used. In dynamic late fusion weights are calculated only once for the usage of all sensors at the same time. When the user deselects a sensor, the corresponding weight is set to 0. The remaining weights are normalised, so that the sum of all weights is 1 again.

Chapter 4

Sensor Fusion in State Estimation

The following chapter deals with the problem of estimating a hidden state over time in a dynamic system using a series of observations from multiple sensors. State estimation problems occur when a state in a system cannot be measured directly or when the measurement quality is insufficient for a proper estimation. For such problems it is characteristic that the state changes over time and that one has access to a series of observations that are related to the hidden state. A common solution is the Bayes filter which estimates the a-posteriori probability for the state given all available observations, up to a certain point in time. The Bayes filter consists of two modes. In the "state transition" a probabilistic prediction is made for the next possible state based on the current state. In the "state evaluation" this prediction is corrected with the help of newly available observations. Since an analytical closed-form solution for the Bayes filter only exists in rare cases, particle filtering as well-known approximation technique will be used throughout this work.

The problem of state estimation will be investigated in the application of indoor localisation. The aim of indoor localisation is to find and track the position of a person inside a building using a variety of sensors. Thus, the state to be estimated is the person's position that changes with every move. For this, the same sensors are used as in Chap. 2. In addition, Wi-Fi, step and turn detection, barometer information and the user's input are integrated as sensor measurements. The main contributions presented in this chapter are the overall design of a complete indoor localisation system, the development of observations models for the walking behaviour of a person, the integration of the user's feedback and the avoidance of wrong heading information.

4.1   Recursive Density Estimation

In recursive density estimation, also known as Bayesian filtering, the goal is to estimate the a-posteriori density

$$p(\mathbf{q}_t \mid \mathbf{o}_{1:t}), \tag{4.1}$$

where

$$\mathbf{q}_t = (q_1, q_2, \dots, q_N)^T \tag{4.2}$$

is a N-dimensional vector representing the state at time t and

$$\mathbf{o}_{1:t}^i = \{\mathbf{o}_{t'}^i \mid 1 \leq i \leq n; 0 \leq t' \leq t\} \tag{4.3}$$

is a series of observations starting from time 1 until time t. Every observation can come from M different sensors and is related to the current state $\mathbf{q}_t$ (see Fig. 4.1). The observation vector is denoted as

$$\mathbf{o}_t^i = \left(o_1^i, o_2^i, \dots, o_M^i\right)^T \ . \tag{4.4}$$

An obvious solution to solve the state estimation problem would be to use Bayes rule, so that

$$p(\mathbf{q}_t \mid \mathbf{o}_{1:t}) = \frac{p(\mathbf{o}_{1:t} \mid \mathbf{q}_t) p(\mathbf{q}_t)}{p(\mathbf{o}_{1:t})} \ . \tag{4.5}$$

However, this direct solution suffers from the problem that for every point in time all measurement values must be available. Consequently, memory and computational requirements grow with every new incoming measurement value. Updating the posterior recursively avoids these disadvantages. If $p(\mathbf{q}_{t-1} \mid \mathbf{o}_{1:t-1})$ is available at $t-1$, then with the Chapman-Kolmogorov equation the prior at time $t-1$ is given by

$$p(\mathbf{q}_t \mid \mathbf{o}_{1:t-1}) = \int p(\mathbf{q}_t \mid \mathbf{q}_{t-1}) \ p(\mathbf{q}_{t-1} \mid \mathbf{o}_{1:t-1}) \ d\mathbf{q}_{t-1} \ , \tag{4.6}$$

where the assumption holds that the process is Markovian and thus the current state $\mathbf{q}_t$ only relies on the previous state $\mathbf{q}_{t-1}$, so that

$$p(\mathbf{q}_t \mid \mathbf{q}_{t-1}, \mathbf{o}_{1:t-1}) = p(\mathbf{q}_t \mid \mathbf{q}_{t-1}) \ . \tag{4.7}$$

Further transformations [44] lead to

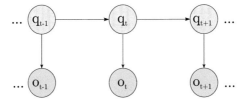

Figure 4.1: The current state $\mathbf{q}_t$ only depends on the previous state $\mathbf{q}_{t-1}$. Each state comes along with an observation $\mathbf{o}_t$ which build a series of observations $\mathbf{o}_{1:t}$ over time.

$$p(\mathbf{q}_t \mid \mathbf{o}_{1:t}) = \frac{p(\mathbf{o}_{1:t} \mid \mathbf{q}_t)p(\mathbf{q}_t)}{p(\mathbf{o}_{1:t})} \tag{4.8}$$

$$= \frac{p(\mathbf{o}_{1:t-1}, \mathbf{o}_t \mid \mathbf{q}_t)p(\mathbf{q}_t)}{p(\mathbf{o}_{1:t-1}, \mathbf{o}_t)} \tag{4.9}$$

$$= \frac{p(\mathbf{o}_t \mid \mathbf{o}_{1:t-1}, \mathbf{q}_t)p(\mathbf{o}_{1:t-1} \mid \mathbf{q}_t)p(\mathbf{q}_t)}{p(\mathbf{o}_t \mid \mathbf{o}_{1:t-1})p(\mathbf{o}_{1:t-1})} \tag{4.10}$$

$$= \frac{p(\mathbf{o}_t \mid \mathbf{o}_{1:t-1}, \mathbf{q}_t)p(\mathbf{q}_t \mid \mathbf{o}_{1:t-1})p(\mathbf{o}_{1:t-1})p(\mathbf{q}_t)}{p(\mathbf{o}_t \mid \mathbf{o}_{1:t-1})p(\mathbf{o}_{1:t-1})p(\mathbf{q}_t)} \tag{4.11}$$

$$= \frac{p(\mathbf{o}_t \mid \mathbf{q}_t)p(\mathbf{q}_t \mid \mathbf{o}_{1:t-1})}{p(\mathbf{o}_t \mid \mathbf{o}_{1:t-1})} \tag{4.12}$$

$$= \eta p(\mathbf{o}_t \mid \mathbf{q}_t)p(\mathbf{q}_t \mid \mathbf{o}_{1:t-1}) \ . \tag{4.13}$$

In Eq. (4.8) Bayes rule is used while Eq. (4.9) is derived by extracting $\mathbf{o}_t$ out of the observation series $\mathbf{o}_{1:t}$. In Eq. (4.10) the chain rule (general product rule) is applied. In Eq. (4.11) again Bayes rule is used so that

$$p(\mathbf{o}_{1:t-1} \mid \mathbf{q}_t) = \frac{p(\mathbf{q}_t \mid \mathbf{o}_{1:t-1})p(\mathbf{o}_{1:t-1})}{p(\mathbf{q}_t)} \ . \tag{4.14}$$

Finally, in Eq. (4.13) Markov's independence assumption [216] that observations are only dependent on the current state

$$p(\mathbf{o}_t \mid \mathbf{o}_{1:t-1}, \mathbf{q}_t) = p(\mathbf{o}_t \mid \mathbf{q}_t) \tag{4.15}$$

is applied. Lastly, η is a normalising constant that will be left out since it is not dependent on the current state. Using Eq. (4.6) in Eq. (4.13) finally results in:

$$p(\mathbf{q}_t \mid \mathbf{o}_{1:t}) = \underbrace{p(\mathbf{o}_t \mid \mathbf{q}_t)}_{\text{likelihood}} \int \underbrace{p(\mathbf{q}_t \mid \mathbf{q}_{t-1})}_{\text{transition}} \ \underbrace{p(\mathbf{q}_{t-1} \mid \mathbf{o}_{1:t-1})}_{\text{recursion}} \ d\mathbf{q}_{t-1} \ . \tag{4.16}$$

A special case arises at the beginning of the estimation process when no observations are available. The initial distribution at time 1 is also known as the prior $p(\mathbf{q}_0)$ and replaces $p(\mathbf{q}_{t-1} \mid \mathbf{o}_{1:t-1})$ at time $t = 1$.

Looking at Eq. (4.16) one can identify three essential parts:

Likelihood: The likelihood $p(\mathbf{o}_t \mid \mathbf{q}_t)$ relates the sensor measurements to a given state and indicates if a predicted state matches the current observations.

Transition: With the transition probability $p(\mathbf{q}_t \mid \mathbf{q}_{t-1})$ the next state $\mathbf{q}_t$ is estimated based on the current state $\mathbf{q}_{t-1}$. The state transition usually is subject to certain constraints, e.g. physical laws that influence the possibility of future states.

Recursion: The recursion part $p(\mathbf{q}_{t-1} \mid \mathbf{o}_{1:t-1})$ contains all information up to time $t-1$.

4.2   Sequential Monte Carlo

Only in special cases an analytical closed form solution for Eq. (4.16) is available. If the posterior and the transition probabilities are assumed to be Gaussian, then an optimal solution can be calculated by the Kalman filter [122]. A less restrictive and widely used method is particle filtering, also known as Sequential Monte Carlo (SMC) method [9, 35, 82, 81, 61, 62] which allows to model distributions that exhibit multi-modalities and which can handle non-linearities in the state and observation models.

Particle filters are an implementation of the recursive Bayes filter which approximate the posterior distribution with a set of weighted samples. The underlying principle relies on the fact that a probability distribution $p(\mathbf{x})$ over a random variable $\mathbf{x}$ can be approximated by N samples $\mathbf{x}^i$ drawn from $p(\mathbf{x})$ with

$$p(\mathbf{x}) \approx \sum_{i=1}^{N} \delta(\mathbf{x} - \mathbf{x}^i) \ , \qquad (4.17)$$

where $\delta(\cdot)$ denotes the Dirac delta function. With this, the expected value of a function f with respect to a probability distribution is

$$\mathbb{E}(f) = \int_{\mathcal{X}} f(\mathbf{x})p(\mathbf{x})d\mathbf{x} \qquad (4.18)$$

and can be approximated with a set of random samples $\mathbf{x}^i$ drawn from p as the sum

$$\mathbb{E}(f) \approx \frac{1}{N} \sum_{i=1}^{N} f(\mathbf{x}^i) \qquad (4.19)$$

under the assumption that the number of samples $N \to \infty$ [8].

The bottleneck in this approach is the prerequisite that one can draw samples from the required probability distribution. While this might be the case for specific distributions like the Gaussian (e.g. using the Box-Muller method), sampling from an arbitrary distribution can become a difficult problem. A popular approach to address the sampling problem is *importance sampling*.

The idea of importance sampling is to introduce a proposal distribution $\pi(\mathbf{x})$ from which it is easy to draw samples from and that is non-zero in all regions where $p(\mathbf{x})$ is non-zero. With this Eq. (4.18) can be rewritten as

$$\mathbb{E}(f) = \int_{\mathcal{X}} f(\mathbf{x}) \frac{p(\mathbf{x})\pi(\mathbf{x})}{\pi(\mathbf{x})} d\mathbf{x} = \int_{\mathcal{X}} f(\mathbf{x})w(\mathbf{x})\pi(\mathbf{x}) d\mathbf{x} \qquad (4.20)$$

and Eq. (4.19) as

$$\mathbb{E}(f) \approx \frac{1}{N} \sum_{i=1}^{N} \frac{p(\mathbf{x}^i)}{\pi(\mathbf{x}^i)} f(\mathbf{x}^i) \qquad (4.21)$$

$$= \frac{1}{N} \sum_{i=1}^{N} w^i f(\mathbf{x}^i) \ . \qquad (4.22)$$

The term $\frac{p(\mathbf{x}^i)}{\pi(\mathbf{x}^i)}$ is also known as importance weight w^i. Finally, one needs to make sure that $\sum_{i=1}^{N} w^{(i)} = 1$ with

$$\hat{w}^i = \frac{w^i}{\sum_{j=1}^{N} w^j} \qquad (4.23)$$

so that

$$\mathbb{E}(f) \approx \frac{1}{N} \sum_{i=1}^{N} \hat{w}^i f(\mathbf{x}^i) \ , \qquad (4.24)$$

where $\mathbf{x} \sim p$. In order to apply importance sampling in the introduced above recursive framework, $p(\mathbf{q}_t \mid \mathbf{o}_{1:t})$ can be rewritten as

$$p(\mathbf{q}_t \mid \mathbf{o}_{1:t}) = \frac{1}{N} \sum \delta(\mathbf{q}_t - \mathbf{q}_t^i) \qquad (4.25)$$

$$\mathbb{E}(f_t) = \int f(\mathbf{q}_t) p(\mathbf{q}_t \mid \mathbf{o}_{1:t}) \qquad (4.26)$$

$$= \frac{1}{N} \sum f(\mathbf{q}_t^i) \ . \qquad (4.27)$$

However, since it cannot be assumed that $p(\mathbf{q}_t \mid \mathbf{o}_{1:t})$ is a distribution from which it is easy to sample from, importance sampling can be used, so that

$$p(\mathbf{q}_t \mid \mathbf{o}_{1:t}) = \frac{1}{N} \sum_{i=1}^{N} \hat{w}_t^i \delta(\mathbf{q}_t - \mathbf{q}_t^i) \ . \qquad (4.28)$$

The empirical distribution of p can then be represented by the set of weighted samples

$$\Upsilon_t = \left\{ \mathbf{q}_t^i, \hat{w}_t^i \right\} \quad . \tag{4.29}$$

When the importance function can be written as

$$\pi(\mathbf{q}_{1:t} \mid \mathbf{o}_{1:t}) = \pi(\mathbf{q}_t \mid \mathbf{q}_{1:t-1}, \mathbf{o}_{1:t-1})\pi(\mathbf{q}_{1:t-1} \mid \mathbf{o}_{1:t-1}) \quad , \tag{4.30}$$

then it is possible to rewrite the weighting of Eq. (4.24) in a recursive form [60], so that

$$w_t^i \propto w_{t-1}^i \frac{p(\mathbf{o}_t \mid \mathbf{q}_t^i)p(\mathbf{q}_t^i \mid \mathbf{q}_{t-1}^i)}{\pi(\mathbf{q}_t^i \mid \mathbf{q}_{1:t-1}^i, \mathbf{o}_{1:t})} \quad . \tag{4.31}$$

However, this variant, known as Sequential Importance Sampling (SIS) filter, suffers from the problem of sample degeneracy. Sample degeneracy occurs because only a few or even only a single sample are assigned the complete weight [157, 55]. To avoid this problem, a resampling step can be introduced after every importance sampling step or whenever a certain criterion is fulfilled. One common criterion is to check if the effective sample size

$$N_{\text{eff}} = \frac{1}{\sum_{i=1}^{N_{\Upsilon_t}} (w_t^i)^2} \tag{4.32}$$

falls below a threshold $N_{\text{eff,t}}$ [132]. Resampling removes particles with small weights and accentuates samples with large ones by selecting samples $\mathbf{q}_t^i$ with replacement proportional to their weight w_t^i from Υ_t. The weights of all samples are set equally to $\frac{1}{N_{\Upsilon_t}}$. Besides encountering the degeneracy problem, computational resources are also saved because samples with small weights, and therefore only limited contribution to the overall estimation, will vanish in the resampling step. Multinomial [199], residual [157] and systematic resampling [131] are among the most popular resampling algorithms, each coming with its own computational complexity and variance. While resampling encounters the problem of sample degeneracy, it also introduces a loss of sample diversity by selecting high-weighted samples in a preferred way [35, 83]. Finally, a careful decision must be made about the proposal distribution since it has a large influence on the variance and the performance of the particle filter. A common solution is to assume the proposal distribution to be equal to the prior

$$\pi(\mathbf{q}_t \mid \mathbf{q}_{1:t-1}, \mathbf{o}_{1:t}) = p(\mathbf{q}_t \mid \mathbf{q}_{1:t-1}) \quad , \tag{4.33}$$

so that the denominator in Eq. (4.31) is cancelled out and only

$$w_t^i \propto w_{t-1}^i p(\mathbf{o}_t \mid \mathbf{q}_t^i) \tag{4.34}$$

remains. This version is also known as Condensation algorithm [111, 110] and will be used throughout this work. The pseudo code for the Condensation algorithm is described in Algorithm 1.

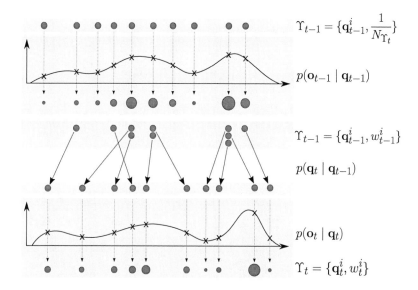

$$\Upsilon_{t-1} = \{\mathbf{q}_{t-1}^i, \frac{1}{N_{\Upsilon_t}}\}$$

$$p(\mathbf{o}_{t-1} \mid \mathbf{q}_{t-1})$$

$$\Upsilon_{t-1} = \{\mathbf{q}_{t-1}^i, w_{t-1}^i\}$$

$$p(\mathbf{q}_t \mid \mathbf{q}_{t-1})$$

$$p(\mathbf{o}_t \mid \mathbf{q}_t)$$

$$\Upsilon_t = \{\mathbf{q}_t^i, w_t^i\}$$

Figure 4.2: Schematic description of the Sampling Importance Resampling (SIR) algorithm. At the beginning a sample set Υ_{t-1} with equal weights is available. Applying the likelihood function $p(\mathbf{o}_{t-1} \mid \mathbf{q}_{t-1})$ results in a weighted sample set Υ_{t-1}. This set is resampled proportional to its weight and distributed according to $p(\mathbf{q}_t \mid \mathbf{q}_{t-1})$. Finally, applying the likelihood function $p(\mathbf{o}_t \mid \mathbf{q}_t)$ results in the sample set Υ_t. The figure was adapted from [110].

4.3   Indoor Localisation

Indoor Localisation is the problem of estimating and tracking the position of a person or an object inside a building [262]. A well known solution for the localisation problem for outdoor areas are Global Navigation Systems (GNS) [124] like the American Global Positioning System (GPS), the Russian GLONASS (Globalnaja nawigazionnaja sputnikowaja sistema), or the European system Galileo. GNS use satellites that are constantly emitting signals containing their positional information in the orbit and the timestamp of the signal. When a device on earth receives the signals of at least four different satellites it can combine the information and derive its own position on the surface of the earth. However, the emitted low-energy satellite signals get attenuated by

---

Algorithm 1 Condensation algorithm as realisation of SIR

1: Draw samples $\mathbf{q}_t^i \sim p(\mathbf{q}_0)$ and add to Υ_0 with weight $w_0^i = \frac{1}{N_{\Upsilon_t}}$

2: **for** every timestep t **do**

3:     **for** every sample $\mathbf{q}_{t-1}^i \in \Upsilon_{t-1}$ **do**

4:         Draw new sample $\mathbf{q}_t^i \propto p(\mathbf{q}_t \mid \mathbf{q}_{t-1})$

5:         Calculated weight $w_t^i = p(\mathbf{o}_t \mid \mathbf{q}_t)$ ▶ Importance sampling

6:     **end for**

7:     **for** every weight $w_t^i \in \Upsilon_t$ **do**

8:         $w_t^i = \frac{w_t^i}{\sum_{j=1}^{N_{\Upsilon_t}} w_t^j}$ ▶ Normalise weights

9:     **end for**

10:    $N_{\text{eff}} = \frac{1}{\sum_{i=1}^{N_{\Upsilon_t}} (w_t^i)^2}$ ▶ Calculate effective sample size

11:    **if** $N_{\text{eff}} \leq N_{\text{eff,t}}$ **then**

12:        **for** $1, ..., N_{\Upsilon_t}$ **do**

13:            Draw sample $\mathbf{q}_t^i$ from $\Upsilon_t \propto w_t^i$ ▶ Resampling

14:            $w_t^i = \frac{1}{N_{\Upsilon_t}}$

15:        **end for**

16:    **end if**

17: **end for**

---

obstacles like walls or even windows and thus, make this technique improper for indoor scenarios [129].

In order to enable localisation and navigation within buildings various methods have been studied in the research field of indoor localisation. The next section summarises the most important techniques. This is followed by a comprehensive explanation of a proposed indoor localisation system which is based on Sequential Monte Carlo and the fusion of multiple sensors. Considering the characteristics of the indoor localisation problem, namely that no sensor exists to directly monitor the user's position and the constantly changing position of the user, indoor localisation perfectly fits the problem definition of recursive density estimation [92].

Introduction

Localisation systems can be categorised into three groups: (i) The first group of methods belongs to the category of absolute positioning systems. These systems are currently delivering the highest accuracy but usually require a laborious pre-configuration and set-up. (ii) The second group are relative positioning systems, also known as dead reckoning systems. These types of systems always estimate a new position in relation to a known reference position. Outgoing from the reference position a new location is

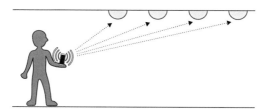

Figure 4.3: The user carries a device that constantly emits a signal that is received by pre-installed receivers.

calculated by adding the assumed covered distance since the last position estimation and the change of direction to the known starting position. For a short duration these system can deliver fine-grained localisation estimations, but are prone to small errors that sum up over a longer period of time. (iii) The third group are hybrid systems that combine the advantages of both systems. Relative positioning delivers short-term but highly accurate estimations which are constantly corrected with the help of absolute positioning systems, so that the system works over a long period of time. The system proposed in this work belongs to the latter category.

Absolute Positioning

Early examples of absolute positioning systems are the Active Badge system [250, 249, 98], the Bat system [5], Cricket [202] and the Dolphin system [77]. To be localised, a person has to wear a badge that emits infrared or ultrasonic signals in regular time intervals. These signals are picked up by pre-installed receivers whose positions in the building are known (see Fig. 4.3). The estimated position corresponds to the location of the device that received the signal. The main drawbacks of this approach are the large number of receivers that have to be installed in the building, and the additional signal emitting device that the user has to carry permanently. Most of today's systems invert this early principle by having instead the user carry a receiver device and installing active senders within the building. Here, especially Wi-Fi plays a major role due to its widespread availability [101, 257, 154]. In the literature, two approaches are predominant for Wi-Fi localisation, namely *signal fingerprinting* and *signal propagation*.

Wi-Fi signal fingerprinting The signal fingerprint method compares the Wi-Fi signals recorded during localisation to a pre-recorded reference database of signals that

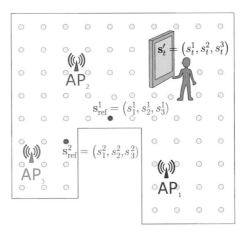

Figure 4.4: In the training phase of Wi-Fi fingerprinting a radio map of the building is recorded which contains several reference measurements at known locations. During localisation, the user's device compares its currently recorded signal strength to the ones of the radio map.

were collected at known locations. Thus, Wi-Fi signal fingerprinting can be split into two phases: the training and the localisation phase.

In the training phase, the received signal strength (RSS) $\mathbf{s}_{\text{ref}}$ is measured at various known reference points in the building and stored in a database which is often called the radio map (see Fig. 4.4). Since the signal of more than one access point (AP) often can be received at any given location, the k-th measurement vector $\mathbf{s}_{\text{ref}}^k$ consists of i different measurements s_i^k stemming from the i individual APs

$$\mathbf{s}_{\text{ref}}^k = \left(s_1^k, s_2^k, \ldots, s_i^k \right)^T \ . \tag{4.35}$$

In the localisation phase the signal vector received $\mathbf{s}_t'$ by the user device

$$\mathbf{s}_t' = \left(s_t^1, s_t^2, \ldots, s_t^i \right) \tag{4.36}$$

at time t is compared to the entries in the radio map. In [14, 188] the position is then estimated using a distance metric $d(\cdot)$, so that the difference between the measured signal and the reference signal is minimised:

$$\mathbf{s}_{\text{ref}}^k = \arg\min_k d(\mathbf{s}_t' - \mathbf{s}_{\text{ref}}^k) \ . \tag{4.37}$$

Thus, the location of the k-th reference point is then the estimated current location of the user. Besides the Euclidean distance that is most often found in the literature,

also the Manhattan distance or cosine similarity are used as distance function [11, 100].
Due to its simplicity, signal fingerprinting is one of the most popular techniques for
Wi-Fi based indoor localisation. However, the quality of RSS measurements is prone
to various influences like the orientation of the user regarding the APs, the way the
user is holding the device or the number of samples taken to construct the radio map
[155]. Probabilistic approaches try to cope with these kinds of effects by modelling the
distribution of the signal in regard to a position. In the probabilistic setup, therefore,
the estimation of the user position $\widehat{\mathbf{x}}$ is redefined as the problem of finding the location
$\mathbf{x}$ that maximises the posterior probability of the location given the vectors of RSSs $\mathbf{s}$
[263, 144]

$$\widehat{\mathbf{x}} = \arg \max_{\mathbf{x}} p(\mathbf{x} \mid \mathbf{s}) \ . \tag{4.38}$$

In general, since the accuracy of the signal fingerprinting approach is highly dependent
on the quality and the number of measurements recorded in the signal map [261], it
suffers from its time-consuming training phase. In addition, the signal map must be re-
recorded whenever changes happen within the building [164]. Those can be significant
constructional modifications like new walls or doors, but often already the presence of
additional persons, furniture or open doors can significantly change the characteristic
of the signal [86]. The main focus of current research in this area is to overcome the
laborious survey of RSS fingerprints. Hereby, one common strategy is to utilise crowd
sourcing, in which users are regularly asked about their approximate position [256, 240,
207]. This position information is then used to build a radio map over a longer period
of time.

Wi-Fi signal propagation Signal propagation avoids the collection of fingerprints
by estimating the RSSs for a given location based on the knowledge of the position of the
APs, the floor map and a physical model of radio wave propagation. The propagation
model has to take effects into account that influence radio waves on their travel between
transmitter and receiver. These effects are known as multipath effects and are the result
of many different physical phenomena like reflection, diffraction, transmission, scattering
or refraction [178, 93].

The most popular propagation model for the indoor area is the log-distance path
loss model [209, 169] which is an adoption of Friis' transition formula [75] for the unob-
structed case,

$$PL(d) = PL(d_0) + 10\gamma \log_{10} \frac{d}{d_0} \ . \tag{4.39}$$

Starting from a reference measurement $PL(d_0)$ that is usually taken in a distance of
$d_0 = 1\text{m}$, the log-distance model Eq. (4.39) estimates the decay of the signal in decibel
dB at a distance d. A crucial factor in Eq. (4.39) is the path loss exponent γ which

is a decline-factor indicating how fast the signal decreases with increasing distance. Especially, γ is dependent on the environment in which the model is applied and can take values like $\gamma = 1.7$ for an open commercial area to $\gamma = 3.5$ for office buildings [218]. The basic log-distance model was extended by [218] and [14] who attached an additional attenuation factor that includes factors like different floor levels or the number of walls.

Another approach to approximate the behaviour of radio waves is the usage of ray tracing models [121, 116]. Since the behaviour of radio waves resembles the ones of light beams, ray tracing models can simulate the travel of a signal and model the above mentioned physical effects like diffraction and diffusion at walls [178]. In other works, the signal strength is approximated by applying Machine Learning methods like curve fitting [241], Artificial Neural Networks [178] or Support Vector Machines (SVM) [31].

Besides Wi-Fi, other sensors are commonly used for absolute positioning. Bluetooth [59, 40, 266, 140, 202, 43] can be treated similarly to Wi-Fi in that a Bluetooth beacon is actively broadcasting messages to its surrounding receivers. Based on the signal strength, the distance between the sender and receiver can be estimated by the same principles that apply to the Wi-Fi scenario. However, the main drawback of this methodology is that the range of a Bluetooth beacon is far below that of an Wi-Fi AP. For that reason, a large number of Bluetooth beacons has to be installed inside a building to enable indoor localisation with this technique. This in turn causes high installation and maintenance costs.

In contrast to this, magnetic measurements collected by a magnetometer do not require any additional hardware setup since they rely on the Earth's magnetic field. The operating principle is alike Wi-Fi fingerprinting. The magnetic field strength is measured at many different locations in the building to obtain a magnetic map of the building. During localisation the measured field strength is compared to the magnetic map [87, 258, 48]. However, due to the numerous magnetic anomalies [145] in an indoor environment, e.g. electric wires, the use of magnetic field measurements can only be used to a limited extent.

Relative Positioning

Relative Positioning, also known as *dead reckoning*, has a long history in navigation [232]. The basic principle of dead reckoning is that, outgoing from a known reference point, every positional change is added to the known starting position which finally leads to a new position estimation [97]. When dealing with indoor localisation for pedestrians, positional changes are usually due to the person walking around in the building. Exceptions to this are cases when elevators and escalators are used which should not be further considered at this point.

Distance Estimation   The activity "walking" can be subdivided into steps, which can be recognised by body-worn sensors like accelerometers. In Chap. 2 various approaches for step detection were described. It has been shown that the number of steps the user has walked since the last update is often sufficient to estimate the person's distance from the reference point [255, 231]. The vast majority of these methods are utilising Inertial Measurement Units (IMUs) which are built into most smartphones.

A different approach to track a user's position is to estimate the exact trajectory of the IMU device in the 3D space [135]. By Newton's law of motion the covered distance can be derived by double integration of the accelerometer signal. However, due to sensor inaccuracies, small errors sum proportionally to the cube of operation time [225] and quickly lead to undesirable meanderings already after a short period of time [74]. This effect can be circumvented by the Zero Velocity Update (ZUPT) [225] which uses the stationary phase during a gait cycle to constrain the velocity error. However, using ZUPT requires the IMU to be mounted directly on the shoe which is impractical in most use cases.

Orientation Estimation   The second pillar of dead reckoning is the determination of the user's movement direction. The obvious solution is to utilise the magnetometer of the IMU as digital compass. But since the magnetometer is highly sensitive to any environmental sources of magnetism, it is thus prone to errors. This is especially true in indoor areas where metallic and electric structures can influence the magnetic field.

If the initial walking direction α is known, the relative heading change $\Delta\alpha$ during the time interval $[t - \Delta t; t]$ in regards to α can be estimated by integrating over the gyroscope signal (see Fig. 4.5):

$$\Delta\alpha = \int_{t-\Delta t}^{t} \theta(t)dt \ . \tag{4.40}$$

Here $\theta(t)$ denotes the measurement value of the gyroscope signal. Computationally, the integration can be done using, for example, the rectangle or trapezoidal rule.

Nevertheless, this is only true if the axis, over which the integral is calculated, is parallel to the user's vertical axis (axis from head to feet). To rotate the phone into the desired position, often hardware vendors provide a rotation matrix that transforms the measurements from a local coordinate system, e.g. the phone's coordinate system to the world coordinate system, e.g. the Earth's coordinate system [192]. Also, in [168] an approach was proposed that fuses different sensors in order to rotate the phone's orientation into the Earth's North-East plane coordinate system.

Similar to the case of step detection, explained in the previous section, gyroscopes suffer from fine measurement inaccuracies which accumulate over time. This prevents the gyroscope from being used for long periods of time.

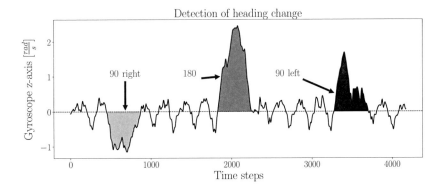

Figure 4.5: Integrating over the gyroscope signal leads to user's change in direction of movement. From left to right, a 90° right turn, a 180° turn, and a 90° left turn are shown in the signal.

To overcome this limitation, the uDirect system proposed in [105, 106] uses a combination of accelerometer, gyroscope and magnetometer. Firstly, the authors determine the device orientation relative to the Earth's coordinate system. This step must be performed while the user is standing and uses the accelerometer in combination with the magnetometer. As the user starts walking, a gait recognition algorithm identifies characteristic segments in the gait, like the swing and the stance phase. With this, the acceleration signal can be aligned with the forward direction of the user.

Another common approach is based on the observation that the user's movement direction is parallel to the axis of the accelerometer with the highest variance, after projecting the signal into the horizontal plane [138, 227, 168]. Hereby, knowledge about the gravity vector is necessary. The gravity vector can be determined by looking for a time interval in which the acceleration signal has almost no variance. This usually is the case when the device rests on the table or the pedestrian stands still without moving the device. In doing so, only the Earth's gravitational force of $9.81\frac{m}{s^2}$ is measured among three axes of the accelerometer [167]. Projecting the accelerometer signal on the gravity vector identifies the share of acceleration that is due to gravitation. The remaining force in the horizontal plane is thus caused by the user's movement. Using Principal Component Analysis (PCA) on the projected signal, the motion direction is approximated by the first eigenvector (see Fig. 4.6).

Floor estimation   In order to measure on which floor level the user is located, the barometer has proven to be a useful sensor. A barometer sensor measures the at-

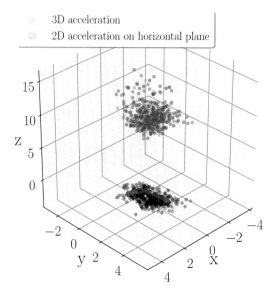

Figure 4.6: After projecting the acceleration signal on the horizontal plane, the largest eigenvector indicates the motion direction of the user.

mospheric pressure of the earth. To estimate the current floor level one can use the knowledge that atmospheric pressure decreases with increasing altitude (see Fig. 4.7) and the relationship between atmospheric pressure and other physical constants that is captured in the barometric formula [113]

$$\rho = \rho_0 \exp\left(-\frac{gM(h - h_b)}{R_0 T_0}\right) \ , \tag{4.41}$$

where

- ρ_0: sea level standard atmospheric pressure (1013.25 hPa)

- g: gravitational acceleration (9.80665 $\frac{m}{s^2}$)

- M: molar mass of air (0.0289644 $\frac{kg}{mol}$)

- h_b: sea level

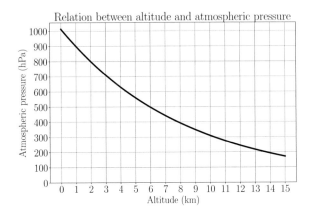

Figure 4.7: Decline of the atmospheric pressure with increasing altitude according to the barometric formula in Eq. (4.41)

- h: altitude above sea level

- R_0: universal gas constant $(8.31447 \frac{J}{mol\,K})$

- T_0: standard temperature $(288.15\,K)$.

The barometer has been successfully used in conjunction with a particle filter in [183] by directly calculating the altitude and mapping this to the known floor elevation. The authors of the work [243] combine the barometer with Wi-Fi fingerprinting and provide an adaptive fusion scheme to cope with the often noisy barometer measurements. As [146] report, one problem that has to be taken in consideration when using a barometer in indoor localisation, is the steadily changing atmospheric air pressure. Consequently, a given floor level cannot be linked to a fixed air pressure on this floor level. In addition, the measurement variations among various devices can cause differences up to 21.6m.

Map information

Pedestrians are naturally subject to certain restrictions when walking within a building. For example, they cannot walk through walls, they have to enter rooms through doors and have to surround obstacles like chairs or tables. Therefore, the usage of a floor map helps to realistically model the pedestrian's behaviour. Often this information is captured in the state transition probability that models the user's movement. For example, [255] use a particle filter in which the state transition eliminates particles

whenever the direct connection between the old and new position intersects a wall.
Similar to this, [29] samples a new position until the transition does not intersect a wall.
This is repeated until the new position is valid, or until a certain number of trials has
been reached. Both methods increase in the worst case the computational complexity
and also "give more probability to a short step" [183].

In order to avoid these disadvantages, it can be beneficial to convert the map into a
graph representation. Voronoi diagrams are a popular choice for this kind of representation and already have a longer history in robotics navigation [149, 73]. In addition,
Voronoi graphs can be constructed automatically from an image of a floor map by a
thinning process [213]. One of the early works in indoor localisation that use this approach was published by [69], where particles are only allowed to move on the edges of
the graph. The work of [103] also transforms the map into a graph and selects a new
position based on a sampled distance and heading, which is similar to [184] who sample
a new position that depends on the reachable number of nodes in the graph. In the
work of [64] the graph also takes stairs and doors into consideration that can be used
as prior knowledge during localisation.

A different usage of the floor map is proposed in [242] and [45]. In their work certain
locations can be treated similar to landmarks. For example, the usage of stairways and
elevators produces a recognisable pattern in the sensor data. Knowing that the user is
currently at such a place drastically narrows down the possibilities for other locations.

4.4 Statistical Models for Multi Sensor 3D Indoor Lo-
calisation

Based on the introduced concepts and ideas form the previous section, the next sections
introduce different models that were developed for indoor localisation. These models
were successfully incorporated in various publications in which the author participated,
namely [135, 134, 133, 66, 65, 70] and [71]. The developed state transition and likelihood models were applied within a Condensation-based particle filter (see Sec. 4.2). A
schematic overview of the system is illustrated in Fig. 4.8.

The models utilise the sensors that are built into a smartphone. These are accelerometers, gyroscopes, and the barometer. Wi-Fi and Bluetooth beacons are used as external
sensors that provide absolute positioning information. All described models can be used
independently of each other. Furthermore, with the independence assumption, the overall likelihood can be formulated as the product of the different models that are chosen

Estimation at $t-1$ Transition model   Observation models   Estimation at t

$p(\mathbf{q}_{t-1} \mid \mathbf{o}_{1:t-1}) \longrightarrow p(\mathbf{q}_t \mid \mathbf{q}_{t-1}) \longrightarrow p(\mathbf{o}_t \mid \mathbf{q}_t) \longrightarrow p(\mathbf{q}_t \mid \mathbf{o}_{1:t})$

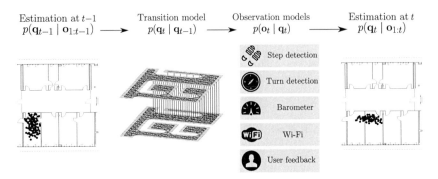

Step detection

Turn detection

Barometer

Wi-Fi

User feedback

Figure 4.8: Overview of the proposed models for an indoor localisation system. Starting from a probability distribution $p(\mathbf{q}_{t-1} \mid \mathbf{o}_{1:t-1})$, a transition model is introduced that uses a graph-based floor map. For the likelihood function different sensor modalities are statistically modelled. This includes the detection of steps and turns, barometer information, Wi-Fi, and the user's feedback. Integrating all of this information leads to a new probability estimation $p(\mathbf{q}_t \mid \mathbf{o}_{1:t})$. All models are used within the framework of recursive density estimation with particle filtering as its realisation.

within an actual implementation of an indoor localisation system:

$$p(\mathbf{o}_t \mid \mathbf{q}_t) = \prod_i^K p(\mathbf{o}_t \mid \mathbf{q}_t)_i \ , \tag{4.42}$$

where the probability $p(\mathbf{o}_t \mid \mathbf{q}_t)_i$ represents one of the likelihood models, e.g. step detection, turn detection, barometer, Wi-Fi or user feedback.

For each proposed model, the state and observation vectors, $\mathbf{q}_t$ and $\mathbf{o}_t$, need to include different variables. These will be described as needed at the beginning of each of the following paragraphs.

4.4.1   Transition Models

A person's movement is limited by physical laws and by typical human behaviour. For example, humans cannot walk through walls, usually walk in straight lines and with a certain speed. The proposed transition model takes these three points into account by utilising a floor map and incorporating probabilities for walking and standing phases. The floor map is used to restrict state changes to such that are realistic.

Random Graph Transition Model

The following paragraph describes a probabilistic model that allows to draw a new position $(x_t, y_t, z_t, \alpha_t)^T$ based on a previous position $(x_{t-1}, y_{t-1}, z_{t-1}, \alpha_{t-1})^T$. The model was published in [65]. Here, x and y represent the 2D coordinates on a building's floor and z the floor level itself. In addition the user's moving direction α is included in the state. Thus, x, y and α are real numbers, while z is an integer, leading to the state definition

$$\mathbf{q}_t = (x_t, y_t, z_t, \alpha_t)^T, \quad x_t, y_t, \alpha_t \in \mathbb{R}, z_t \in \mathbb{N} \ . \tag{4.43}$$

The original floor map is reflected as a graph, where each node is the centre of a square and each node is connected with an undirected edge to every of its adjacent squares. Squares are only placed at locations that are accessible by the user, e.g. free space. Walls and other obstacles are left out and therefore cannot be accessed. The graph G is represented by all its vertices V and edges E (see Fig. 4.9). Each square is represented by its vertex $v_{x,y,z} \in V$ that lies in the centre of a square. Adjacent squares are connected by an undirected edge e, such that

$$e_{v_{x+i,y+j,z}}^{v_{x,y,z}} \in E, \quad i, j \in \{-s, 0, s\}, i \neq 0 \vee j \neq 0 \ . \tag{4.44}$$

If squares on two different floor levels are connected by each other due to staircases or elevators, an additional vertical edge $e_{v_{x+i,y+i,z'}}^{v_{x,y,z}}$ is introduced.

The next possible position is dependent on the average walking speed of the pedestrian and the time between two updates t and $t-1$. The grid size is a free hyperparameter, but in general a grid size of $s = 20\,\text{cm}$ is a decent choice.

To sample a new position the following steps are necessary:

1. To begin with, a random distance d is drawn from a bimodel distribution according to

$$d \sim k\mathcal{N}(\mu_{\text{walk}}, \sigma_{\text{walk}}^2) + (k-1)\mathcal{N}(\mu_{\text{stand}}, \sigma_{\text{stand}}^2), \quad 0 < k < 1. \tag{4.45}$$

   The distance estimates how far the user can walk in the time span between t and $t-1$. At normal walking speed, humans typically need around 0.5 seconds for every step with an average stride length of 80 cm.

   The estimated distance is given by μ_{walk} with a variance of σ_{walk}^2. The parameter k represents the probability of the user walking. k can either be fixed as a constant throughout the localisation, or estimated dynamically and updated for every new time step. μ_{stand} expresses the distance when standing, which is usually around 0 cm.

2. Based on the starting position $(x, y, z)^T$, the vertex $v_{x,y,z}$ is determined.

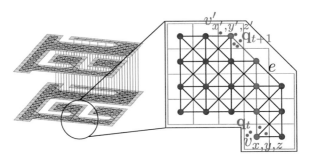

Figure 4.9: On the left side two floors are shown modelled as graph. On the right side a more detailed view shows that each square consists of a vertex and each vertex is connected to its adjacent vertices. The figure was adapted from [65].

3. A random walk on the graph is performed by drawing a next edge $e \sim p(e \mid (x, y, z)^T)$ and subtracting the length of the edge $\|e\|$ from the distance d. This procedure is repeated until $d \leq 0$. In general, pedestrians walk in straight lines and only in rare cases deviate from this behaviour. This can be modelled according to the probability distribution $p(e \mid \mathbf{q}_t)$, by assigning a higher probability to edges that do not alter the walking direction, so that

$$p(e \mid \mathbf{q}_t) = \mathcal{N}(0, \sigma_{\text{dir}}^2) \ . \tag{4.46}$$

Hereby, a normally distributed number is drawn which represents the angle between the predecessor edge e' and the current edge e denoted as $\angle e'e$. The heading α is updated by assigning $\alpha_t = \angle e$.

4. When the last edge was reached, the final position is determined by uniformly drawing a position from the square of the target vertex $v_{x',y',z'}$.

Finally, a special case must be considered when a change is made between two floor levels, since no 2D angle exists between edges that lie "above" each other. To encounter such cases, a high probability is assigned to edges that are connected vertically. To avoid frequent alternations between two floor levels, this model prohibits multiple changes during a single walking simulation.

Incorporating activity recognition   As proposed in [71], a slight modification to the selection of next edges e can be performed if activity recognition is included in the process. The detection of the activities standing, walking and walking stairs up or down, can be incorporated as additional knowledge within the state transition. Edges on the graph that align with the currently detected activity can be favoured by increasing their probability of being selected.

4.4.2   Sensor Models

Wi-Fi

In this work, a probabilistic signal propagation model based on Wi-Fi signals is used as absolute positioning system. The statistical model to incorporate the Wi-Fi signals is based on the publications [66, 65, 71] in which the probability for a position is given by the knowledge about the received signal strength.

The proposed Wi-Fi model requires that the three dimensional position $\varrho = (x, y, z)^T$ is part of the state vector $\mathbf{q}_t$. As observation the received signal strength $\mathbf{s}$ is included into the observation vector $\mathbf{o}_t$. The received signal strength is measured by a device that a user is wearing during the localisation, e.g. a smartphone. Since multiple access points are often available at a given location, the received signal is a composition of multiple different signals, and thus, the signal strength vector $\mathbf{s}$ is defined as

$$\mathbf{s} = (s_1, \cdots, s_n)^T, \;\; s_a \in \mathbb{R} \;\; , \tag{4.47}$$

where s_n is the signal sent from the n-th access point. As will be pointed out in the following description of the method, the location of the access points within the building must be known beforehand. Moreover, for each access point reference measurements must be taken to optimise certain model parameters.

Given a received signal strength $\mathbf{s}$, the task is to estimate the probability $p(\mathbf{s} \mid \varrho)$, which is the probability for a received signal strength given a current position.

The probability $p(\mathbf{s} \mid \varrho)$ can be rewritten as

$$p(\mathbf{s} \mid \varrho) = \frac{p(\varrho \mid \mathbf{s}) \cdot p(\varrho)}{p(\mathbf{s})} \;\; . \tag{4.48}$$

In Eq. (4.48) the probability $p(\varrho)$ describes the a-priori probability of a person being at a certain location in the building. This is especially useful if certain assumptions about a user can be made. For example, an office worker typically stays at his own desk over a longer period of time during the day. The probability $p(\mathbf{s})$ is a normalising constant and can be omitted [212]. If no further knowledge is assumed for $p(\varrho)$ then Eq. (4.48) can be simplified to

$$p(\mathbf{s} \mid \varrho) = p(\varrho \mid \mathbf{s}) \;\; . \tag{4.49}$$

Considering this, the problem now is to estimate a probability for a current measurement given a user's position. This formulation corresponds to the likelihood $p(\mathbf{o}_t \mid \mathbf{q}_t)$ required within the recursive density estimation framework Eq. (4.16).

Based on the log-distance model in Eq. (4.39) a modified model is proposed in [66] that measures the absolute signal strength $P_r(d)$ for a single access point at a distance d by

$$P_r(d) = P_0 - 10\gamma \log_{10} \frac{d}{d_0} + X_\sigma \; . \tag{4.50}$$

Here, P_0 describes a measurement that was carried out at a known distance d_0 from an access point. This is the reason why the position of the access points must be known beforehand. Such a reference measurement is necessary, since the used hardware, antenna and system configuration differs among different use cases [119]. In addition, X_σ is a noise parameter that incorporates unmodelled effects like moving obstacles [67]. Often a Gaussian distribution with a variance σ_{wifi} is chosen as the distribution of X_σ. The parameter γ is a factor that describes the decrease of the signal strength with increasing distance to the access point [220]. However, it should be noted that a single parameter is a large simplification of all the physical effects influencing the signal. For this reason, each access point should have its own γ value.

Using Eq. (4.50) the probability for a signal strength s_a, which is measured at the distance d_a from the a-th access point, is given by

$$p(s_a \mid d_a) = \mathcal{N}(s_a \mid P_0 - 10\gamma \log_{10} \frac{d}{d_0}, \sigma_{\text{wifi}}) \; . \tag{4.51}$$

Reformulating the distance d_a in Eq. (4.51) as the difference between the known position of the access point ϱ_a and the user's position ϱ leads to

$$p(s_a \mid \varrho) = \mathcal{N}(s_a \mid P_0 - 10\gamma \log_{10} \frac{\|\varrho_a - \varrho\|}{d_0}, \sigma_{\text{wifi}}) \; . \tag{4.52}$$

Assuming that the signals of direct access points do not influence each other, statistical indepence among the signals results in

$$p(\mathbf{s} \mid \varrho) = \prod_{a=1}^{n} p(s_a \mid \varrho) \; . \tag{4.53}$$

With a known reference measurement at a known distance, the parameters P_0 and γ are left in Eq. (4.51) as subject of optimisation with respect to

$$(\widehat{P_0}, \widehat{\gamma}) = \arg \min_{(P_0, \gamma)} \sum_{i=1}^{n} (\|P_r(d_i) - s_i\|) \; . \tag{4.54}$$

Finally, due to the fact that wearable devices are equipped with different antennas, the received signal strength will vary among different devices, even if these devices are of the same type and from the same maker [46]. To compensate for this effect, it is suggested to transform the received signal strength relative to the most significant one, which is denoted as s_{max} [245]:

$$s_{\mathrm{max}} = \max_a(s_a), \quad a = \{1, ..., n\} \; , \tag{4.55}$$

which leads to

$$\bar{s}_a = s_a - s_{\mathrm{max}} \tag{4.56}$$

for every received signal strength measurement s_a and a reformulation of the probability to

$$p(\bar{s}_a \mid \boldsymbol{\varrho}) = \mathcal{N}(\bar{s}_a \mid P_0 - 10\gamma \log_{10} \frac{\|\boldsymbol{\varrho}_a - \boldsymbol{\varrho}\|}{d_0}, \sigma_{\mathrm{wifi}}) \; . \tag{4.57}$$

Bluetooth Beacons   Bluetooth beacons are very similar to Wi-Fi signals in that the same physical model of radio signal propagation applies. Bluetooth beacons constantly fire a radio signal into their environment, which can be captured by surrounding receivers. Using the signal propagation model, it is therefore possible to estimate the distance between the sender and the receiver. Knowing the position of the beacons, these sensors can be used as an additional information source in the localisation process. However, this also comes with the drawback that for large buildings many beacons must be installed and maintained.

Barometer

The method to estimate the floor level proposed in this work is based on the publication [65]. At the beginning of the localisation a reference measurement ρ_{ref} of the current atmospheric pressure is carried out. This reference measurement is necessary because the atmospheric pressure changes over time due to weather conditions and internal effects like open windows and therefore is unknown when the localisation starts. It is recommended to take the average of multiple barometer measurements as reference measurement to compensate variations due to sensor instabilities [71].

During localisation a relative atmospheric pressure ρ_t^{rel} is calculated by subtracting the currently measured atmospheric pressure value ρ_t from the reference measurement:

$$\rho_t^{\mathrm{rel}} = \rho_t - \rho_{\mathrm{ref}} \; . \tag{4.58}$$

To simplify further notation, all barometric measurements are assumed to be relative to the reference measurement, so that the superscript "rel" will be left out.

The proposed transition and evaluation models that incorporate the barometer assume that the state $\mathbf{q}_t$ contains the current floor level z and an estimation of the relative atmospheric pressure $\widehat{\rho}_t$. The observation vector $\mathbf{o}_t$ includes the currently measured relative atmospheric pressure ρ_t.

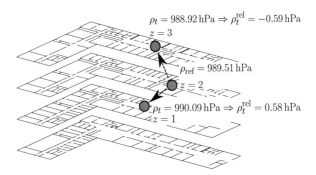

Figure 4.10: All barometer measurements are relative to an initial reference measurement ρ_{ref}, which was recorded on the second floor level in this example. Each increase or decrease of the floor level changes the estimated barometer value, which is given by the barometric formula. Changing into the first or third floor causes a change in the barometer measurements relative to the reference measurement made at the beginning of the localisation process.

Transitioning from state $\mathbf{q}_{t-1}$ to $\mathbf{q}_t$ is done by drawing a new estimated barometric pressure value for the next step from the distribution

$$p(\mathbf{q}_t \mid \mathbf{q}_{t-1}) = \mathcal{N}(\widehat{\rho}_t, \sigma^2_{t,\mathrm{baro,trans}}) \ , \tag{4.59}$$

where $\sigma^2_{t,\mathrm{baro,trans}}$ denotes the variance of the distribution. The variance should be chosen large enough so that transitions from one floor to another floor are possible.

The probability for an estimated measurement value $\widehat{\rho}_t$ is given by

$$p(\mathbf{o}_t \mid \mathbf{q}_t)_{\mathrm{baro}} = \mathcal{N}(\widehat{\rho}_t \mid \rho_t, \sigma^2_{t,\mathrm{baro, \ eval}}) \tag{4.60}$$

with a mean at ρ_t and the modelled sensor noise given by the variance $\sigma^2_{t,\mathrm{baro, \ eval}}$.

Step Detection

The following paragraph describes how the recognition of steps helps to track positional changes of a user and in which way this information can be included statistically into the localisation process using recursive state estimation. Methods introduced in this section were also published in the papers [134, 65, 66, 71].

The main purpose of step detection is to gather the information whether and how far the user has moved during the last time interval. With this knowledge, the distance d can be determined between the position $(x_t, y_t, z_t)^T$ in state $\mathbf{q}_t$ and the position

$(x_{t-1}, y_{t-1}, z_{t-1})$ in state $\mathbf{q}_{t-1}$. Formally, information about steps are included in the
observation vector $\mathbf{o}_t$ as a counting variable, indicating how many steps were detected
in the time interval since the last update.

The step information can be integrated in two ways in a recursive density estimation:
Firstly, it can be used within the likelihood function $p(\mathbf{o}_t \mid \mathbf{q}_t)$ to estimate the probability
for a hypothetical state $\mathbf{q}_t$. However, because a positional change always considers the
current and the previous state $\mathbf{q}_t$ and $\mathbf{q}_{t-1}$, it is mandatory to include the previous state
$\mathbf{q}_{t-1}$ into the likelihood function, so that $p(\mathbf{o}_t \mid \mathbf{q}_t)$ extends to $p(\mathbf{o}_t \mid \mathbf{q}_t, \mathbf{q}_{t-1})$. Secondly,
the knowledge whether a person has walked or not in the last time interval, can be used
as additional assistance within the state transition. In this case, the detection of a step
determines the distance for the state transition from $\mathbf{q}_{t-1}$ to $\mathbf{q}_t$. If the observation of a
step is integrated into the transition, then the standard transition probability $p(\mathbf{q}_t \mid \mathbf{q}_{t-1})$
changes to $p(\mathbf{q}_t \mid \mathbf{q}_{t-1}, \mathbf{o}_t)$.

The following derivation is the theoretical basis for the integration of the previous
state $\mathbf{q}_{t-1}$ into the likelihood function and the observation vector $\mathbf{o}_t$ into the transition
probability[134]:

$$p(\mathbf{q}_t \mid \mathbf{o}_{1:t}, \mathbf{q}_{t-1}) \tag{4.61}$$

$$= \frac{p(\mathbf{q}_t, \mathbf{o}_{1:t}, \mathbf{q}_{t-1})}{p(\mathbf{q}_{t-1}, \mathbf{o}_{1:t})} \tag{4.62}$$

$$= \frac{p(\mathbf{q}_t, \mathbf{o}_t, \mathbf{o}_{1:t-1}, \mathbf{q}_{t-1})}{p(\mathbf{q}_{t-1}, \mathbf{o}_{1:t-1}, \mathbf{o}_t)} \tag{4.63}$$

$$= \frac{p(\mathbf{o}_{1:t-1}) p(\mathbf{q}_{t-1} \mid \mathbf{o}_{1:t-1}) p(\mathbf{q}_t \mid \mathbf{o}_{1:t-1}, \mathbf{q}_{t-1}) p(\mathbf{o}_t \mid \mathbf{q}_t, \mathbf{o}_{1:t-1}, \mathbf{q}_{t-1})}{p(\mathbf{o}_{1:t-1}) p(\mathbf{q}_{t-1} \mid \mathbf{o}_{1:t-1}) p(\mathbf{o}_t \mid \mathbf{q}_{t-1}, \mathbf{o}_{1:t-1})} \tag{4.64}$$

$$= \frac{p(\mathbf{q}_t \mid \mathbf{o}_{1:t-1}, \mathbf{q}_{t-1}) p(\mathbf{o}_t \mid \mathbf{q}_t, \mathbf{o}_{1:t-1}, \mathbf{q}_{t-1})}{p(\mathbf{o}_t \mid \mathbf{o}_{1:t-1}, \mathbf{q}_{t-1})} \tag{4.65}$$

$$= \frac{1}{\alpha} \cdot p(\mathbf{q}_t \mid \mathbf{o}_{1:t-1}, \mathbf{q}_{t-1}) p(\mathbf{o}_t \mid \mathbf{q}_t, \mathbf{o}_{1:t-1}, \mathbf{q}_{t-1}) \tag{4.66}$$

$$= \frac{1}{\alpha} \cdot p(\mathbf{q}_t \mid \mathbf{o}_{1:t-1}, \mathbf{q}_{t-1}) p(\mathbf{o}_t \mid \mathbf{q}_t, \mathbf{q}_{t-1}) \tag{4.67}$$

$$= \frac{1}{\alpha} \cdot p(\mathbf{o}_t \mid \mathbf{q}_t, \mathbf{q}_{t-1}) \int p(\mathbf{q}_t \mid \mathbf{q}_{t-1}, \mathbf{o}_{1:t-1}) p(\mathbf{q}_{t-1} \mid \mathbf{o}_{1:t-1}) d\mathbf{q}_{t-1} \tag{4.68}$$

$$= \frac{1}{\alpha} \cdot p(\mathbf{o}_t \mid \mathbf{q}_t, \mathbf{q}_{t-1}) \int p(\mathbf{q}_t \mid \mathbf{q}_{t-1}, \mathbf{o}_{t-1}) p(\mathbf{q}_{t-1} \mid \mathbf{o}_{1:t}) d\mathbf{q}_{t-1} \tag{4.69}$$

In Eq. (4.62) the definition of the conditional probability is applied, and Eq. (4.64) results
by using the Multiplication Theorem of probabilities. Equation (4.65) is the reduced
form of Eq. (4.64). Since the denominator does not depend on the current state, it
is a constant and, therefore, denoted as α in Eq. (4.66). Markov's assumptions leads
to $p(\mathbf{o}_t \mid \mathbf{q}_t, \mathbf{q}_{t-1})$ because the current observation does not depend on the previous

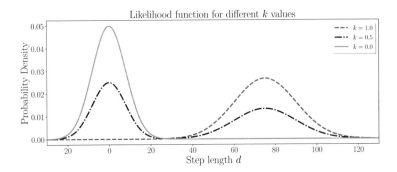

Figure 4.11: Probability density for different values of k in $p(\mathbf{o}_t \mid \mathbf{q}_t, \mathbf{q}_{t-1})_{\text{step}}$. When a step was detected ($k = 1$) the peak of the probability is centred around a typical step length of 75cm.

observation and thus can be omitted in $p(\mathbf{o}_t \mid \mathbf{q}_t, \mathbf{o}_{1:t-1}, \mathbf{q}_{t-1})$. Applying the Total Law of Probability for $p(\mathbf{q}_t \mid \mathbf{q}_{t-1}, \mathbf{o}_{1:t-1})$ finally results in $p(\mathbf{q}_t \mid \mathbf{q}_{t-1}, \mathbf{o}_t)$.

In [135, 134, 65] the likelihood function $p(\mathbf{o}_t \mid \mathbf{q}_t, \mathbf{q}_{t-1})$ was proposed to adopt a mixture model that has two components. The first component considers the case where the user has made a step in the last time interval, while the second component looks at the case where the user has stopped,

$$p(\mathbf{o}_t \mid \mathbf{q}_t, \mathbf{q}_{t-1})_{\text{step}} = \underbrace{k \cdot X_{\text{step}}}_{\text{walking}} + \underbrace{(1 - k) \cdot X_{\text{stand}}}_{\text{standing}} \ . \tag{4.70}$$

The variations of the step lengths are modelled as random variables X_{step} or, if no step was detected as X_{stand}, respectively. The parameter k is a weighting factor, indicating the proportion of every mixture component in regards to the total distribution. In a deterministic setting, the step detection process sets $k = 1$ if a step was detected, and $k = 0$ otherwise. However, as shown in [134], there is also the possibility to assign k the probabilistic output of a step detection algorithm. In this case, k takes a value in the interval $[0; 1]$. Assuming both mixture models, for example to be Gaussian, results in

$$p(\mathbf{o}_t \mid \mathbf{q}_t, \mathbf{q}_{t-1})_{\text{step}} = k\mathcal{N}(d_{\text{obs}} \mid d_{\text{step}}, \sigma_{\text{step}}^2) + (1 - k)\mathcal{N}(d_{\text{obs}} \mid d_{\text{stand}}, \sigma_{\text{stand}}^2) \ , \tag{4.71}$$

where the mean of the first Gaussian is given by d_{step} with variance σ_{step}^2 and d_{stand} and σ_{stand}^2 for the case when no step was detected, respectively. The resulting distribution is visualised in Fig. 4.11, where a mean step length of $d_{\text{step}} = 75$cm with a variance $\sigma_{\text{step}}^2 = 15$cm is assumed. In case the user was not walking during the last time interval, $d_{\text{stand}} = 0$ with a variance of $\sigma_{\text{step}}^2 = 8$cm. The variable d_{obs} denotes the covered distance between a state $\mathbf{q}_t$ and $\mathbf{q}_{t-1}$. Thus, using the probability function $p(\mathbf{o}_t \mid \mathbf{q}_t, \mathbf{q}_{t-1})_{\text{step}}$, states $\mathbf{q}_t$ are assigned a high probability if the distance d between the positition at time t and the position t correspond with the result of the step detection. If a single step was detected by the step detection process, then the next position should consequently also be approximately a single step ahead. If no step was detected, the distance should be close to zero.

As described earlier, the step observation can also be integrated into the transition probability, which in turn becomes $p(\mathbf{q}_t \mid \mathbf{q}_{t-1}, \mathbf{o}_{t-1})$. Hereby, the transition probability determines a new position given the current position together with the knowledge about the user's movement. Following the model for the likelihood function, the transition probability can be formulated similarly as

$$p(\mathbf{q}_t \mid \mathbf{q}_{t-1}, \mathbf{o}_t)_{\text{step}} = k\mathcal{N}(d_{\text{walk}}, \sigma_{\text{walk}}) + (k-1)\mathcal{N}(d_{\text{stand}}, \sigma_{\text{stand}}) \ . \tag{4.72}$$

In essence, this transition probability samples a distance from a mixture distribution that is similar to Eq. (4.71), where each mixture component again represents one of the two cases "walking" and "standing". Assuming no further knowledge about the user's walking direction α, the user's new position is given by

$$x_t = d\cos(\alpha_t) \tag{4.73}$$
$$y_t = d\sin(\alpha_t) \ . \tag{4.74}$$

The distribution of the newly sampled position is represented in Fig. 4.12. However, if map information is included in the transition step, the transition probability given by Eq. (4.72) can also be used within a more complex model, e.g. the random transition graph model in Sec. 4.4.1.

Turn Detection

Using the gyroscope sensor, changes in the user's movement direction can be tracked and included in the density estimation process. Basic techniques to accomplish this have already been introduced in Sec. 4.3. Despite the fact that smartphones are commodity hardware, most research works assume that the user does not change the position of the smartphone during navigation. Since this assumption rarely holds in real-world scenarios, next a technique is introduced that detects sudden orientation changes of a phone and, thus is able to avoid the integration of faulty measurements values. This method was published together with previous models in [65]. It assumes heading information α_t to be included in the $\mathbf{q}_t$ and heading change information in the observation $\mathbf{o}_t$.

Gyroscope Based Heading Estimation   A simple state evaluation function is given by

$$p(\mathbf{o}_t \mid \mathbf{q}_t, \mathbf{q}_{t-1}) = \mathcal{N}(\alpha_t - \alpha_{t-1} \mid \Delta\alpha_t, \sigma_{\text{heading}}^2) \ . \tag{4.75}$$

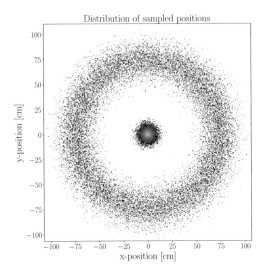

Figure 4.12: Sampling from the transition probability given by a step detection process like in Eq. (4.72) results in the shown distribution of samples. Since no further heading information is given, the samples that are drawn in the case of walking build a circle around the centre. The centre itself represents the case of standing.

The heading $\Delta\alpha$ denotes the measurement value that comes from integrating over the gyroscope (see Sec. 4.3 and Fig. 4.5) and is used as mean value of the normal distribution. $\Delta\alpha_t - \Delta\alpha_{t-1}$ corresponds to the difference of estimated headings in the current and previous state $\mathbf{q}_t$ and $\mathbf{q}_{t-1}$, respectively. With this, a new state is assigned a high probability if its heading change compared to the previous state is approximately the measured heading change by the gyroscope.

Avoidance of Erroneous Measurements   As already stated, the estimation of the heading change is only applicable in cases in which the phone's position is stable. To relax this assumption a method is proposed to encounter erroneous heading estimations. The basic idea is to reduce the confidence in the heading estimation whenever the system recognises an orientation change of the phone that is not related to a walked turn. Such a change could, for example, be caused by the user who is putting the phone back into his pocket, or receives a phone call. An obvious example is the rotation of the smartphone from portrait view to landscape view. While the gyroscope measures a 90°

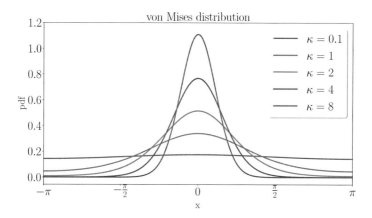

Figure 4.13: The von Mises distribution, also known as *circular normal* [27, Chap. 2]. The distribution becomes almost uniform for small κ values.

turn, in fact only the orientation of the phone changes but not necessarily the user's walking direction.

Since the motion axis is the axis in the phone's coordinate system that is parallel to the user's walking direction, any orientation change of the phone also comes together with a motion axis change. This assumption holds as long as the phone's orientation is not changed at the same the user changes also his walking direction. Based on this observation, gyroscope readings can be neglected if they are measured during an occurrence of a motion axis change.

To incorporate such a mechanism, the von Mises distribution is utilised [27, Chap. 2]. The von Mises distribution is comparable to the Gaussian distribution, but circularly defined on the interval $[-\pi; \pi]$. The probability density of the von Mises distribution is given by

$$f_{\text{mises}}(x \mid \mu, \kappa) = \frac{e^{\kappa \cos(x-\mu)}}{2\pi I_0(\kappa)} \ , \tag{4.76}$$

where I_0 is the modified Bessel function of order 0. The mean is given by μ and κ is a variance parameter. The smaller κ, the more uniform the von Mises distribution becomes (see Fig. 4.13). To accomplish a mechanism that removes erroneous heading measurements, firstly a motion axis is determined with the approach by [138, 167, 227] that was already presented in Sec. 4.3. The motion axis at time t will be denoted as $\mathbf{m}_t$, and is defined as the phone axis to which the user is walking parallel to. The angle ϕ_t

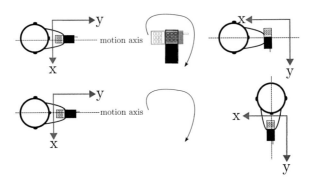

Figure 4.14: The top image shows the situation when the user turns his phone by 90°. Before the turn, the motion axis is parallel to the phone's y-axis, after the turn it is parallel to the phone's x-axis. In contrast, the bottom image shows a situation where the user walks a 90° turn. Here, the motion axis stays parallel to the phone's y-axis. In both situations the gyroscope measures a 90°.

between two consecutive motion axis $\mathbf{m}_t$ and $\mathbf{m}_{t-1}$ is given by

$$\cos \phi_t = \frac{\mathbf{m}_t \cdot \mathbf{m}_{t-1}}{\|\mathbf{m}_t\|\|\mathbf{m}_{t-1}\|} \quad , \tag{4.77}$$

and since the direction of the motion axis is not important at this point, the final angle difference is given by

$$\Delta \phi_t = \min(\pi - \phi_t, \phi_t) \quad . \tag{4.78}$$

Additionally, the following heuristic function is defined

$$\kappa = f_\kappa(\Delta \phi_t) = \frac{1}{e^{\Delta \phi}} \quad , \tag{4.79}$$

which determines a κ value in dependence of the motion axis change $\Delta \Phi_t$. By this, whenever the motion axis shows a significant change, the resulting κ value ensures that the corresponding von Mises distribution becomes almost uniform. Because uniform distributions do not contain any information, the estimated heading changes are ignored for this time step. The final likelihood function is therefore given by:

$$p(\mathbf{o}_t \mid \mathbf{q}_t, \mathbf{q}_{t-1}) = f_{\mathrm{mises}}(\alpha_t - \alpha_{t-1} \mid \Delta \alpha_t, \kappa) \quad . \tag{4.80}$$

User Feedback

In the paper [133] a statistical model is proposed that interrogates the user about characteristics within his field of vision and incorporates the user's answer as additional information source into the localisation system. A question is triggered by the system whenever the localisation system meets a criteria for inaccuracy. Such situations can occur when the localisation mainly relies on dead reckoning and looses its precision over time or in case of ambiguities that cannot be resolved. With the user's answer the system should then have enough information to run the localisation accurately again. Integrating the user as additional "sensor" allows to gather information that is easily obtainable by a human but would be hard or impossible to gather in an automatic fashion. For example, the user can be asked if he sees a specific object in the room he is currently in. While such a question can be easily answered by a person, it would require a camera or other sensors to answer this question otherwise. One disadvantage, which naturally arises from such a "question-and-answer" system is the intrusiveness for the user. With that in mind the proposed system should consult user's as rarely as possible.

Questioning a user or another system about specific information is historically known as mediation [58] and has its roots in the database domain to integrate knowledge form various sources [254]. In the literature the usage of user feedback can often be found when building up a radio map for Wi-Fi localisation. Here several papers propose to ask the user about his current position and in turn mark the estimated location together with the received measurement strength [26, 30, 160, 159, 179]. One dilemma that incurs with such an approach is that, especially in localisation, it cannot be assumed that the user has any knowledge about his position. Otherwise he would not need the localisation process anyway. The authors of [130] ask the user to label a specific location if their system considers it to be interesting for the specific user. One criteria for an interesting place is the amount of time the user stays at this location. In the work of [191], user feedback is formulated in a graph-based framework called human-assisted graph search (HumanGS). The semantic information about the questionable matter is represented as directed acyclic graph. The questions are, however, created upfront which restricts the usage of this method for real-time usage.

Feedback Evaluation   The system triggers a question to gather additional information when it reaches a level of uncertainty. The user's answer is then integrated as probability of being at one or more specific rooms. The system asks questions about characteristics of a place or room. An example is the question "if the room, the user is in, is a lecture hall". The answer can be either positive or negative. If the answer is positive, the user confirms the assumption of the system. If the answer is negative the system can exclude the specific rooms.

Figure 4.15: A typical situation for a multimodal distribution. The localisation system was not able to distinguish through which door the user entered the room so that the position estimation is split up in two different locations. The set of particles is forming two clusters that are fitted to Gaussian distributions $\mathcal{N}_1$ and $\mathcal{N}_2$. The mean values are drawn as circle and square, respectively. The system tries to resolve the situation by asking the user for additional information about the location.

Four different cases were identified that can occur whenever the system is interrogating the user:

- The user confirms the assumption of the system: If the user answers positively to the system's question, the system gathers the information that the user is located in the places to which the question was referring to. Consequently, this provides additional information.

- The user denies the assumption of the system: A negative answer to the system's question has as consequence that the system can exclude the location that the question was referring to.

- The user provides wrong information: This case might arise if the user deliberately or unintentionally gives an incorrect answer. Hereby, the system will not gather any additional information. However, it is difficult to identify such an instance.

- The system provides wrong information: This situation can occur if the system relies, for example, on outdated or wrong information.

The last two cases presuppose that it is acutally possible to identify them. However, this is usually not the case. For this reason, the proposed statistical model treats these incidents similar to "sensor noise", meaning that they introduce a small amount of uncertainty to the location information.

Following the model proposed by the authors of [133], the likelihood function based on the answer of the user can be formulated as

$$p(\mathbf{o}_t \mid \mathbf{q}_t) = \underbrace{k_1(I_a\mathcal{U}(\mathcal{A}) + I_a\mathcal{U}(\mathcal{B}))}_{\text{position information}} + \underbrace{(k_2 + k_3)\mathcal{U}(\mathcal{M})}_{\text{noise}} \ . \tag{4.81}$$

Here, the set of all possible locations within the building is denoted as $\mathcal{M}$. Questions by the system refer to a set of locations of $\mathcal{A}$. This means that, if the user answers positively to a question, the system can limit possible locations to all locations within the set $\mathcal{A}$. Contrary, questions that are answered negatively, provide information about the locations that are not included in $\mathcal{A}$, which are denoted as $\mathcal{B} = \mathcal{M} \setminus \mathcal{A}$. The places denoted by $\mathcal{A}, \mathcal{B}$ and $\mathcal{M}$ are indicated in Fig. 4.16. The indicator function I_a is defined as

$$I_a = \begin{cases} 1, & \text{if answer } a \text{ is positive} \\ 0, & \text{if answer } a \text{ is negative} \end{cases} \tag{4.82}$$

with a as an answer of the user to a system's question.

The statistical model in Eq. (4.81) that evaluates a current position given the user's answers can be split in two major parts. The front part contains the actual information about the position. If the user's answer is positive then all positions that are part of $\mathcal{A}$ are assigned a uniform weight. On the other hand, if the answer is negative all position in $\mathcal{B}$ and, therefore, outside $\mathcal{A}$, are equally weighted. Finally, the last term $\mathcal{U}(\mathcal{M})$ represents an uniform probability for all possible positions. This term can be treated similarly to sensor noise in that it models the situations in which either the system or the user provides incorrect information and thus, no additional information is gathered. All terms are combined in a mixture distribution with components proportional to k_1 and $(k_2 + k_3)$, respectively. Setting reasonable values for k_1, k_2 and k_3 depends on the trustworthiness of the users, e.g. if the user will consciously provide wrong information, and the error rate of the question generating system.

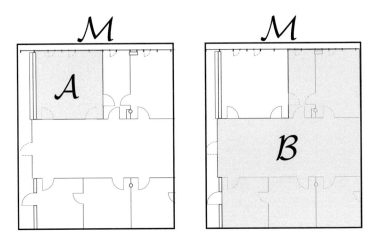

Figure 4.16: Questions of the system correspond to places marked by the area denoted as $\mathcal{A}$, while other places are marked as $\mathcal{B}$. All possible locations within the map are given by the set $\mathcal{M}$.

Uncertainty measurement   Using particle filtering as realisation of the recursive density estimation provides a probability density in form of weighted samples for the positions. Based on this density, a current position must be estimated. One solution for this is to fit a Gaussian distribution to the complete particle set. However, a Gaussian fitting only makes sense if all particles are close to each other. Or said differently, if the distribution is in fact Gaussian and especially, no multimodalities occur.

To identify multimodalities in the distribution, a Gaussian mixture model (GMM) with two Gaussians is fitted to the particle set. Since every Gaussian provides its own mean, covariance and weight, an uncertainty can be defined as a divergence of the two mean values. If multimodalities occur like in Fig. 4.15, this will be visible as two Gaussians whose mean values are far away from each other. In this case it might make sense to trigger a question to gather more information.

Question generation   An open issue up to this point is in which way questions are generated so that enough information is gained from the user to solve ambiguities like illustrated in Fig. 4.15. The question generation approach proposed in [133] is based on a semantic map that represents the building and in particular the objects that are within the different rooms. Based on this knowledge, questions can be asked by the system, such as whether the user sees a red picture hanging on the wall. Since the question generator interacts with the localisation system, it has knowledge of the possible locations the user might be. Using this information together with the semantic map, a decision tree chooses a question about an object among all the different objects in the eligible rooms with the goal to narrow down possible locations. One disadvantage, however, is the construction of the semantic map since it requires a detailed and up to date knowledge of discriminable objects within all rooms.

4.5 State Estimation and Classification

The upcoming section introduces recursive density estimation as classification method in the area of gesture recognition. The data that is used here is recorded by multiple sensors that are attached to the user's body. Gesture recognition is very similar to activity recognition in that human movements should be assigned to semantic meaningful class labels. However, the expressiveness of a gesture is also characterised by the way it is executed. In particular, parameters like the speed and the intensity of a gesture can add information to it. These are, similar to indoor localisation, variables that cannot be measured directly. Recursive density estimation, however, offers again a framework to infer such parameters from the recorded sensor data. By designing the state q_t appropriately, it is in addition possible to do classification concurrently to the parameter estimation. This principle of using recursive density estimation together with classification was demonstrated in the past by [28] and [56].

4.5.1 Gesture recognition

In gesture recognition the aim is to interpret movements of a user's hands, arms, face, head and body in order to improve the interaction between humans and machines [166]. Hence, common applications for gesture recognition can be found when interacting with large displays, robotics, but also augmented and virtual reality applications [211]. In addition, it offers some interesting challenges:

- **User independence**: If possible, systems should be built for user-independent utilisation. Alternatively, a user-dependent model can be trained during some sort of calibration phase. The downside is the additional effort that a user would have to put into this calibration.

- **Natural gesture**: The system should be able to recognise a gesture, even if it is executed in different ways. In particular, parameters such as speed and intensity should be freely chosen by the user. Furthermore, these parameters can be used for additional functionalities in gesture recognition. As [36] has shown in his work, the speed of a gesture can be used to control with which speed a music system plays back a song.

- **Gesture spotting**: Typically, only a small part of a user's movement is in fact a gesture. Hence, often gesture recognition algorithms require a specific signal to start the recognition system. This usually feels unnatural and should preferably be detected automatically by the system (gesture spotting).

- **Delay-free recognition**: Delays between the execution of a gesture and its recognition by the system disturb the natural interaction between both. Hence, the system should react as soon as possible to a recognised gesture.

The literature offers a variety of approaches to gesture recognition [166]. To narrow down the existing work we exclude papers that focus on video data as input and instead focus on gesture recognition algorithms that are based on time series data, e.g. accelerometer.

To address these issues different approaches have been proposed in the literature. The uWave system [156] is based on data from a three-axis accelerometer. Incoming data are compared to examples of gestures that were recorded during a training phase. The comparison is made using Dynamic Time Warping (DTW) as similarity measure. To avoid classifying all users' movements as potential gestures, the authors introduced a similarity threshold. If the distance between the incoming data and all stored template gestures does not reach this threshold, the system classifies the data as unknown gesture. In order to start the system, the user has to press and hold a button while executing a gesture. In paper [7] gestures from the training dataset are clustered using DTW and Affinity Propagation. Newly observed data is firstly compared to all cluster centres and then to all members of the most similar cluster by projecting the gestures into a lower dimensional space. This solves the problem of gestures having variable length and decreases computational complexity. The authors of [47] approach the problem of gesture spotting by comparing the variance of the signal to a manually set threshold. In addition, the variance is also used to detect the intensity of the gesture. Ward et al. [251] combine the classification results from a microphone and accelerometer whereby classification is performed with a Hidden Markov Model (HMM). Whenever the likelihood across all possible gestures falls below a certain threshold, the investigated data segment is classified as the null class. The work of [120] introduces a two-stage approach for gesture classification. In a first step, segments of data within the time series are searched that could potentially include a gesture while in a second step classification is done by a HMM model.

In addition to gesture classification, the method of Caramiaux [36] does also track parameters like the speed, scale and rotation of the hand with which the gesture is per-

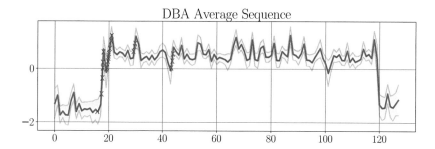

Figure 4.17: Shown is a template gesture calculated with the DBA method. The principle of the proposed approach is to use particle filtering to estimate the gesture class and especially which part of a gesture a user is currently performing. Particles that correspond to the current sensor observation will receive a higher weight and thus, match with regions in a template gesture of high probability. Particles are illustrated as red crosses here. Coloured areas above and below the average sequence show the region that is one standard deviation above and below the average sequence values.

formed. As a basis for this, the method of [28] is adopted, which uses the Condensation algorithm for the classification of gestures by adding additional continuous and discrete variables to the state and defining appropriate state transition and observation models. The basic idea is to increase the weights of particles that match with a particular gesture class and concurrently have similar latent parameters like the speed and scale with which the gesture is performed.

4.5.2 Method Overview

The algorithm presented here and published in [148] also uses particle filtering for gesture recognition similar to the work of Caramiaux [36], but extends certain components such as the training phase and the particular models within the state estimation. More specifically, gesture templates are calculated as the average sequence of all sequences from the training set using DTW Barycentric Averaging (DBA). These templates are used as comparison basis for the incoming data stream. In particular, each new sensor data is related to the values of the average gesture. If the incoming sensor value matches values of the average gesture the probability for the corresponding gesture class is increased (see Fig. 4.17). The history of sensor observations and their correspondence to gesture templates is available as prior probability at each new time step, while the transition model moves particles forward along the template gesture.

4.5.3   DTW Barycentric Averaging (DBA)

DBA is an algorithm which iteratively computes the average of a set of time series and which was proposed by Petitjean in [195, 194]. As the name suggests, DTW is used as underlying distance metrics which was already introduced in Chap. 2.2.3. As a quick reminder, DTW aligns two sequences in such a way that the distance between these sequences is minimised even if the sequences are of unequal length or distorted. The result is a cost matrix $\mathbf{C}$ that contains all distances between all pairs of elements of the two sequences. The optimal distance is given by the warping path, and the sum of costs along the warping path gives the final DTW distance. DBA builds averages of multiple sequences as follows:

Given a set S of N training sequences by

$$S = \left\{ \mathbf{o}_{1:\tau_1}^1, \mathbf{o}_{1:\tau_2}^2, \ldots, \mathbf{o}_{1:\tau_n}^n \ldots \mathbf{o}_{1:\tau_N}^N \right\} \; , \tag{4.83}$$

DBA computes the average sequence

$$\mathbf{o}_{1:\tau_\phi}^\phi = \left\{ o_1^\phi, \ldots, o_\varphi^\phi, \ldots o_{\tau_\phi}^\phi \right\} \tag{4.84}$$

by applying the following steps [195]:

1. The average sequence $\mathbf{o}_{1:\tau_\phi}^\phi$ is initialised with a length τ_ϕ which must be chosen appropriately. One strategy is to use the average length of all sequences in S. The initial values of $\mathbf{o}_{1:\tau_\phi}^\phi$ can be selected randomly. The average sequence of iteration i is denoted as $\mathbf{o}_{1:\tau_\phi}^\phi$, while the average sequence of the iteration $i+1$ will be denoted as $\widehat{\mathbf{o}}_{1:\tau_\phi}^\phi$.

2. The DTW distances between the average sequence $\mathbf{o}_{1:\tau_\phi}^\phi$ and all sequences $\mathbf{o}_{1:\tau_n}^n$ from the set S are calculated. Consequently, this results in N DTW distances, N warping paths and N DTW cost matrices. Using these results, all associations between the average sequence and training sequences in S are determined. An association between elements of two sequences is given, if the combination of the r-th element o_r^ϕ of the average sequence and the p-th element o_p^i from the training sequence are part of the warping path that forms the particular DTW distance. Using these associations an "association table" $\mathbf{A}$ can be built that contains one row for each element of the average sequence (τ_ϕ rows) and each row holds the elements that are associated with one element of $\mathbf{o}_{1:\tau_\phi}^\phi$. Basically, the association table tells about which elements of the training sequences contribute to a specific element of the average sequence. Hence, the φ-th entry of the association table is notated as $A[\varphi]$ and the entries form a list $\mathbf{A}[\varphi] = \left\{ o_y^x \mid x \in \{1, \ldots, N\}, y \in \{1, \ldots, \tau_x\}, (o_\varphi^\phi, o_y^x) \in \mathbf{p} \right\}$, where $\mathbf{p}$ is the DTW warping path (see Fig. 4.18 for a detailed example).

3. Since multiple elements of a sequence in S can contribute to a single element of the average sequence, the value of an element of the average sequence is given by the barycentric average of the associated elements given in the association table $\mathbf{A}$. Given a row $\mathbf{A}[\varphi]$ of the association table with α number of entries by $\mathbf{A}[\varphi] = \{a_1, \ldots, a_\alpha\}$, where each a_i denotes one associated element, the value of the φ-th element of the new average sequence $\widehat{\mathbf{o}}^\phi_{1:\tau_\phi}$ is given by:

$$o^\phi_\varphi = \frac{\sum_i^\alpha a_i}{\alpha} \ . \tag{4.85}$$

At the same time, the standard deviation for each element of the average sequence can be calculated with

$$\sigma^\phi_\varphi = \frac{1}{\alpha} \sum_{i=1}^\alpha (a_i - \mu_\varphi)^2 \ . \tag{4.86}$$

4. Step 2 and step 3 are repeated until a convergence criterion is reached.

In order to find the best average sequence, in this work the DBA algorithm is started N times - one time for every sequence in S. With every new start the average sequence is initialised in step 1 as one of the sequences of S. The final average sequence $\mathbf{o}^\phi_{1:\tau_\phi}$ is given by the average sequence that minimises the sum of all DTW distances between itself and all sequences in S. An example for an averaged sequence is shown in Fig. 4.19.

Timestamp conversion A final step has to be performed to prepare the average sequence for later use in the particle filter algorithm. Given the nature of the DBA algorithm, multiple elements of a single training sequence can contribute to a single element of an average sequence. One example is given in Fig. 4.18, where the middle training sequence contributes with three elements to one element of the average sequence. This raises the problem that the calculated average sequence does not have any valid timestamps. To illustrate this, one can imagine an extreme example of a training sequence having only three elements, sampled every 0.33 seconds. The corresponding timestamps are then $0.33, 0.66$ and 1.0. If the average sequence has a length that is much longer, which timestamps should be assigned to the elements of the average sequence? More informally, one could also say that the training sequence is performed "faster" or "slower" than the average sequence. To counter this problem a special transformation is proposed:

- Let z^φ_n be the number of associations between one element o^ϕ_φ of the average sequence and all elements of the n-th training sequence $\mathbf{o}^n_{1:\tau_n}$.

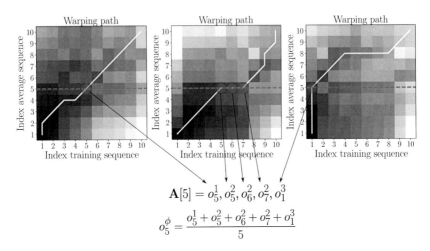

$$\mathbf{A}[5] = o_5^1, o_5^2, o_6^2, o_7^2, o_1^3$$

$$o_5^\phi = \frac{o_5^1 + o_5^2 + o_6^2 + o_7^2 + o_1^3}{5}$$

Figure 4.18: Associations between an average sequence and three training sequences are shown. Exemplarily, the associations to the fifth element o_5^ϕ of the average sequence is depicted. The first training sequence (left side) is only associated with its own fifth element o_5^1 to o_5^ϕ, the second training sequence (middle) has in total three associations o_5^2, o_6^2, o_7^2, while the last training sequence again only has a single association o_1^3. The final list represents one row in the association table. These elements build the entry $\mathbf{A}[5]$ of the association table. The final element o_5^ϕ of the average sequence is given by the barycentric average.

- Let $r_{t_n}^n$ be the number of associations between one element $o_{t_n}^n$ of the n-th training sequence and all elements of the average sequence $\mathbf{o}_{1:\tau_\phi}^\phi$.

With this, a matrix $\mathbf{V}$ can be defined where the entry in the n-th row and φ-th column is given by

$$\mathbf{V}[n, \varphi] = \begin{cases} z_n^\varphi, \text{if } z_n^\varphi > 1 \\ \frac{1}{r_{t_n}^n}, \text{if } r_{t_n}^n > 1 \\ 1, \text{else} \end{cases} . \tag{4.87}$$

Essentially, each entry of the matrix provides information about how many elements of the training sequences are used to derive one element of the average sequence. If $\mathbf{V}[n, \varphi] > 1$ then the average sequence is faster than the particular sequence. Contrary, if $\mathbf{V}[n, \varphi] < 1$ then the average sequence is slower than the particular sequence. An example is given in Fig. 4.20. Using Eq. (4.87) a vector $\mathbf{v}$ of length τ_ϕ can be defined

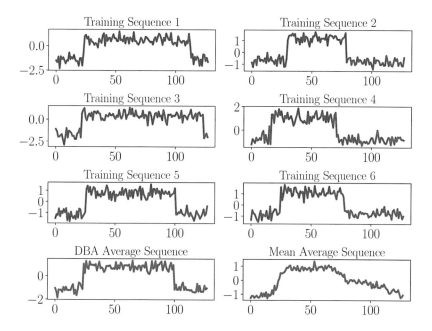

Figure 4.19: Example of applying DBA to six sequences (shown in the top three rows) which results in one average sequence (shown in the last row on the left side). For comparison, on the bottom right the average sequence using the mean of all sequences is illustrated. It is clearly visible that DBA captures the shape of the sequences much better.

using all N training sequences by

$$\mathbf{v}[\varphi] = \frac{1}{N} \sum_{i=1}^{N} \mathbf{V}[i, \varphi] \tag{4.88}$$

which are the mean values of the columns of $\mathbf{V}$. With this newly created vector it is now possible to map the indices of the average sequence back to the sampling time which is usually given in seconds. This timestamp will be denoted with T_Φ^ϕ and represents the timestamp of an average sequence for the φ-th element. The conversion is defined as

$$T_\varphi^\phi = \begin{cases} 0, & \text{if } \varphi = 0 \\ T_{\varphi-1}^\phi + \mathbf{v}(\varphi - 1)\Delta T, & \text{else} \end{cases} . \tag{4.89}$$

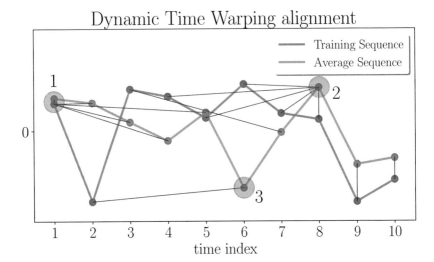

Figure 4.20: The image shows the DTW alignment of an average and a training sequence. The warping path for these sequences is shown in Fig. 4.18 on the right side. The red circle denoted as 1 gives an example of $r_{t_n}^n = 4$, one element of the training sequence is linked to four elements of the average sequence. Hence, these four elements take the same amount of time like the single training sequence element. The second red circle illustrates $z_n^\varphi = 5$ since the the average sequence element is linked with five other elements. Finally, circle 3 is a direct one-to-one mapping.

Here, ΔT is given in seconds and denotes the time interval between two consecutive sensor samplings which can be derived from the sensor frequency.

Extension to multi-dimensional case The previous description only considers the one-dimensional case, e.g. a single sensor was used. To extend the methodology to the multi-sensor case, the average sequence $\mathbf{o}_{1:\tau_\phi}^\phi$ is considered as a matrix instead of a vector given by

$$\mathbf{O}^\phi = (\mathbf{o}_{1:\tau_{\phi_1}}^{\phi_1}, \ldots, \mathbf{o}_{1:\tau_{\varphi_k}}^{\phi_k}, \ldots, \mathbf{o}_{1:\tau_{\phi_K}}^{\phi_K}) \qquad (4.90)$$

and each vector can be written as

$$\mathbf{o}_\varphi^\phi = (o_\varphi^{\phi_1}, \ldots, o_\varphi^{\phi_k}, \ldots o_\varphi^{\phi_K})^T \ , \qquad (4.91)$$

where K is the total number of sensors and each coordinate $o_\varphi^{\phi_k}$ of the vector $\mathbf{o}_\varphi^\phi$ represents the φ-th average element of the average sequence of the k-th sensor.

4.5.4 Gesture Recognition with Particle Filtering

With the calculated average gestures, a real-time gesture recognition can now be carried out, whereby the already introduced particle filter is used. The goal is to derive at any time an estimation of the probability of which gesture the user is currently executing and in particular which temporal portion of a gesture is being executed. In the following, all relevant parts that are needed to identify gestures using particle filtering will be described.

Training phase   Using DBA to generate average sequences of multiple time series, for each gesture class a template gesture is created from the data collected in the training phase. More specifically, for a number of κ gestures and u users, each user generates r_κ repetitions of a specific gesture. The data is obtained by N different sensors. For each gesture a multi-dimensional template gesture $\mathbf{O}_g^\phi$ is created that will be used throughout all models.

State definition   In order to be able to classify sensor data into appropriate gesture classes, the following state definition is used

$$\mathbf{q}_t = (\Omega_t, T_t^k) \ , \tag{4.92}$$

where Ω_t represents the estimated gesture class at time t while the variable T_t^k denotes the timestamp of the template gesture of class Ω_k. Using this state definition, the goal is to find out which gesture and especially which part of the gesture the user is currently executing.

The initial state is given by

$$\Omega_t = \mathcal{U}(\Omega) \tag{4.93}$$
$$T_t^k = \mathcal{N}(0, \sigma_k) \tag{4.94}$$

which is given by a uniform distribution across all possible gesture classes and setting the timestamp normally distributed at the beginning of the template gesture of class k. Consequently, particles are distributed among all possible gesture templates and placed approximately at the beginning of these.

Transition model   The state $\mathbf{q}_{t+1}$ is defined by the transition

$$T_t^k = T_{t-1}^k + \alpha_k \Delta T \ , \tag{4.95}$$

where α_k is a normally distributed random variable and ΔT is the time interval between two updates of the sensor. Essentially, this transition model is moving the estimated timestamp forward along the specific gesture template. The gesture class of a particle stays always the same, so that $\Omega_t = \Omega_{t-1}$.

Observation model   The observation model assigns a weight to each particle that reflects its accordance with the current sensor measurements. Given the sensor measurement o_t^n at time t from the n-th sensor the weight w_t^i is given by

$$w_t^i = \prod_{n=1}^{N} \mathcal{N}(o_t^n \mid o_\varphi^\phi, \sigma_\varphi^\phi) \ , \tag{4.96}$$

where σ_φ^ϕ is the standard deviation of the average sequence calculated in Eq. (4.86). Essentially, incoming sensor data is compared to the values of the average sequences at time index φ. As described previously, this time index must be converted to real-valued timestamps by Eq. (4.89). These derived weights are finally normalised so that they sum to 1.

Resampling   A resampling is introduced whenever the effective sample size falls below a pre-defined threshold. This procedure was already introduced in Eq. (4.32). A low effective sample size can be especially observed, whenever particles do not cover an area of an average gesture sequence that the user is currently performing. Therefore, a small number of new particles is spread across the complete average gesture before the actual resampling step takes place. With this a higher number of regions of the probability space is covered.

Classification   In a final step, the weighted particles are used to derive an estimation of the gesture the user is currently performing. For this, the weights of all particles that represent the same gesture class are summed up:

$$p(\Omega_k) = \sum_{i=1}^{N_{\Upsilon_t}} \widehat{w_t^i}, \text{if } \Omega_t = k \ , \tag{4.97}$$

in which $\widehat{w_t^i}$ is the normalised weight, Ω_t is the gesture class represented in the $\mathbf{q}_t$ and Υ_t is the set of all particles.

The estimated class $\widehat{\Omega_t}$ is given by searching for the maximum value of all $p(\Omega_k)$ values

$$\widehat{\Omega_t} = \underset{\Omega_k}{\mathrm{argmax}}\, p(\Omega_k) \ . \tag{4.98}$$

In order to avoid meaningless classification results, especially at the beginning of a performed gesture, it is suggested to assign the class "unknown" to the classification result until a heuristic threshold was exceeded.

Chapter 5

Experiments

In the upcoming chapter the experimental results for the proposed methods are described. This includes a detailed evaluation of the feature learning approach using different datasets. Further, indoor localisation was tested on data from a real large-scale environment. The gesture recognition approach was tested on standard benchmark datasets.

5.1 Experimental Results for Feature Learning

This section starts with an overview of the implementation details of the general activity recognition framework. In addition, the utilised training and testing datasets are introduced. This is followed by an evaluation of the system's performance regarding the activity recognition accuracy and its computational time. Finally, the system performance is evaluated by comparing individual sensors against each other and the influence of different fusion schemas on the result is examined.

5.1.1 Implementation Details of our Activity Recognition System

In Fig. 5.1 the general hardware setup is illustrated for the implemented activity recognition system. The test persons are equipped with a smartphone (Google Nexus 5X), a smartwatch (Microsoft Band 2 [165]) and smartglasses (JINS Meme [118]). These devices are used to track the movements of the user's body, hand and head, respectively. In doing so, the following data is collected (abbreviations for a sensor are denoted in brackets):

1. **Smartphone** From the smartphone acceleration (sp-acc), gyroscope (sp-gyro), grav-

	sp-acc, sp-gyro sp-grav, sp-linacc	sp-mag	sw-acc, sw-gyro	sg-acc
Sampling rate (Hz)	200	50	67	20
Window size w_{sub}	128	64	64	32
Sliding size λ_{sub}	8	4	4	1

Table 5.1: Summary of all sensor parameters.

ity (sp-grav), linear acceleration (sp-linacc) and magnetometer (sp-mag) data are gathered.

2. **Smartwatch** The smartwatch is used to collect acceleration (sw-acc) and gyroscope measurements (sw-gyro) measured directly at the hand.

3. **Smartglasses** The only data that is obtained from the smartglasses is an acceleration signal (sg-acc).

The sampling rates of the acceleration, gyroscope, gravity and linear acceleration of the smartphone are 200Hz while the sampling rate of the smartphone's magnetometer is 50Hz. The smartwatch collects the acceleration and gyroscope signal with 67Hz and the smartglasses their acceleration data with 20Hz (see table 5.1). As introduced in Fig. 3.2 for the general framework, wearable devices - in this example smartwatch and smartglasses - send their data firstly to the smartphone using a Bluetooth 4.0 connection. Following, RabbitMQ [203] as an open source implementation of the AMQP protocol is used to transfer the data from the smartphone to the central server over a Wi-Fi connection. The server is a cheap commodity computer (Intel NUC NUC5i5RYK) with Core i5-5250U 1.6GHz, 16GB of RAM, 450GB HDD and a Linux system (Debian 4.8.4-1). On this server activity recognition is performed on the incoming data. Here, for each type of sensor a single codebook is constructed. This means that since each sensor type consists of three dimensions (x-, y-, and z-axis), codewords are extracted from three-dimensional subsequences. This procedure also helps to capture correlations among the three axes. Hence, clustering is performed by concatenating three sensor dimensions into a single $3w_{\mathrm{sub}}$-dimensional vector, where w_{sub} is the length of a subsequence. The elements 1 to w_{sub} of this new vector represent the data of the x-axis, elements w_{sub} to $2w_{\mathrm{sub}}$ the y-axis and $2w_{\mathrm{sub}}$ to $3w_{\mathrm{sub}}$ the z-axis, respectively. The same subsequence representation is also used for the codebook construction and codeword assignment without further modifications. The hyper-parameters for the codebook construction were chosen based on preliminary experiments as $w_{\mathrm{sub}} = 128$ and $\lambda_{\mathrm{sub}} = 8$ for sp-acc, sp-gyro, sp-grav and sp-linacc, $w_{\mathrm{sub}} = 64$ and $\lambda_{\mathrm{sub}} = 4$ for the sensors sp-mag, sw-acc and sw-gyro, and $w_{\mathrm{sub}} = 32$ and $\lambda_{\mathrm{sub}} = 1$ for sg-acc. The main criteria to choose

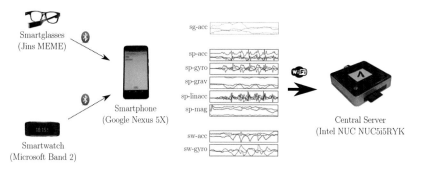

Figure 5.1: An overview of an implementation of the general framework for activity recognition. The data from smartglasses and smartwach is sent via Bluetooth to the smartphone. From there the collected data is sent to a central server where the activity recognition takes place.

these parameters is to have a sufficient amount of subsequences for a window size of five seconds which is the size of a sequence w_{seq} on which the final classification is performed. Using these parameters a sequence of the sensors sp-acc, sp-gyro, sp-grav and sp-linacc will consist of around 100 subsequences, while a sequence of sensor sp-mag will be represented by 45 subsequences and sensors sw-acc, sw-gyro and sg-acc by 60 subsequences each. The total number of codewords N_ψ is set to a value of 1024 for every sensor type. As described in Chap. 3, the parameters w_{seq}, w_{sub}, λ_{sub} and N_ψ are the only parameters that must be set manually. In addition, no pre-processing like e.g. signal noise filtering, was performed. An overview over the important sensor parameters can be found in table 5.1.

The experiments were performed on 11 activities, namely: 1. lying, 2. sitting, 3. standing, 4. walking, 5. bending, 6. getting up, 7. lying down, 8. pulling hand back, 9. sitting down, 10. standing up, and 11. stretching a hand. For this, a training dataset was created which contains the previously mentioned eight sensor types for in total 145 executions of these activities per user. Hence, a user performed every activity more than 10 times. To collect these data a user was executing one of the activities within a time window of five seconds. Users were asked to perform each activity execution in a different style. For example, the activity lying was done by lying on the back, on the stomach, on the side or changing the lying style during the execution. This variation ensures a wide combination of training data to cope with different use cases in the testing phase. It should also be noted that the labelling of the data was done in a "loosely" way, meaning that the activity only has to be included within the five second window. However, the activity itself does not have to take exactly five seconds. With this approach it is guaranteed that the final feature vector contains subsequences that encompass important parts of the activity. Concurrently, it makes the collection of training data less laborious.

In total 11 SVMs - one for each activity - are trained using the training dataset. However, during the training phase a special adaptation has to be made. The activities lying, sitting, standing and walking are considered here as *static* activities, while the remaining activities are *dynamic* ones. Static activities represent a user's state, whereas dynamic activities represent short movements when the user is currently in a static state. In particular, dynamic activities like stretching a hand can be executed while sitting or lying. Hence, SVMs for static activities should not be trained using all other activities as negative examples. Otherwise it is possible that negative examples include the execution of the particular static activity that should, in fact, be treated as positive example. Thus, only other static activities which are different than the static activity that should be recognised are included in the training set as negative examples. With this it can be guaranteed that the particular static activity is not included twice, as possible and as negative example. This restriction does not apply to dynamic activities since no other activity can include coincidentally another dynamic activity. Using this setup, 11 SVMs are built for all activities.

The performance of the SVMs are tested on a dataset containing 124 executions of the various 11 activities. These activities are executed by the same users but on a different day. As evaluation measure two different metrics are used. The first one is the simple accuracy, which denotes the ratio between correct and incorrect predictions for the 124 test examples. To take into account that some of the static and dynamic activities can occur concurrently, the final prediction for a test example of a static (or dynamic) activity is done by taking the highest SVM score that is obtained among all four static (or seven dynamic) activities. The reason for this is that concurrently occurring activities would otherwise degrade the accuracy result and lead to an underestimation of the the recognition performance. An example for this case is when the user stretches his hand while he is standing and the activity recognition system labels this example as the activity "stretching hand". Even though the SVM outputs a high score for the stretching activity, the score for the standing activity might still be higher since the user is in fact standing. With the described methodology also these cases can be evaluated in a meaningful unbiased way.

As second evaluation measure Average Precision (AP) [161] is used. The AP metric is often used in information retrieval systems where it is usually more important to present the user the most relevant results in an order of importance then the final accuracy. Given a specific target activity, AP considers the difference between the SVM scores that are assigned to all test examples for a target activity. All test examples are

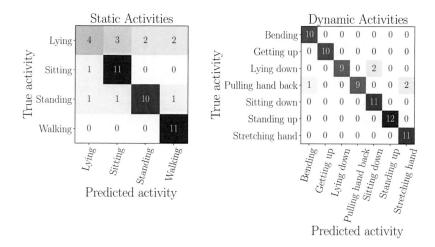

Figure 5.2: The image shows the confusion matrices for static and dynamic activities, respectively. Overall, the system is able to recognise most activities correctly. The main exception to this is the lying activity which gets confused with all other static activities.

ranked according to the SVM score for a specific target activity. Then the precision is calculated for each scored test example given its ranked position. Put differently, the AP metrics approximate the area under the recall-precision curve using the obtained SVM scores. The AP becomes large and therefore better, whenever many text examples labelled with the target activity are ranked higher than test examples labelled with non-target activities. Due to this ranking-based statistical computation, it is not necessary to make a separation between static and dynamic activities. Despite the fact that for some examples of static activities also dynamic activities will be assigned a high SVM score, it can be expected that a good classifier will also assign high SVM scores to the static activity class and puts it also on a higher rank. Thus, the AP metric is typically useful for relative performance comparisons among different methods. To obtain the Mean of APs (MAP), the mean of all APs across the 11 activities is calculated.

5.1.2   Overall Performance Evaluation

The overall system performance applying the early fusion approach and separating between static and dynamic activities as described above, results in an accuracy of 87.1%. In Fig. 5.2 the confusion matrices for static and dynamic activities are illustrated. The

row of each matrix corresponds to the ground truth while the column shows the predicted activities of the algorithm. The main diagonal of a confusion matrix represents
correctly labelled activities. As can be seen in Fig. 5.2, most activities are recognised
with reasonably high accuracy. The only exception to this is the the activity "lying"
which is easily confused with other activities that depend on the user's posture. The
main reason for this is that it is difficult to distinguish between activities that do not
include any movement of the user. The only distinguishing feature that is available in
these cases is the orientation of the sensor, especially the gravity sensor. For example,
given the postures of the activities "standing" and "lying" the orientation of the phone
in the user's pants pockets will be very similar. The reason for the confusion between
"lying" and "walking", however, is not so clear. One possibility might be that the user
has changed his lying position during execution and thus, produces similar patterns to
the "walking" activity.

Besides these, other misclassifications of the system can be considered as reasonable
or sometimes even correct. As shown in the confusion matrix of the dynamic activities,
the activity "pulling hand back" is labelled two times as "stretching hand". However, it
could be observed during the experiments that the user stretched his hand again within
the five seconds window without annotating it appropriately so that both activities
were included in a single training instance. Given this observation, it can be concluded
that the system is able to recognise in detail which activities the user has performed.
However, the importance and difficulty of collecting appropriate training data is also
shown within this example.

In Fig. 5.3 the APs and MAP of the proposed system for all of the 11 activities are
displayed. Although the individual results vary across the activities, the overall system
reaches a high MAP value of 88.8%. Even though APs vary depending on activities,
our system accomplishes a very high MAP value of 88.8%.

The aforementioned results validated the system in an off-line experiment. Following,
the system is tested for the real-time case on the central server (see Fig. 5.1). For this,
for each sensor a buffer is defined that puts the latest incoming data into a queue and
removes the oldest data from this queue. The buffer length for each sensor is fixed at 1500
data points (7.5 seconds) for the sensors sp-acc, sp-gyro, sp-grav and sp-linacc that have
a sampling rate of 200 Hz. For the sensor sp-mag, sw-acc and sw-gyro that sample the
data with 50 Hz the buffer contains 450 data points while it is 6.7 seconds large for the sw-
acc and sw-gyro sensors (67 Hz). Finally, the buffer for the smartglasses' accelerometer
sg-acc, sampling at a rate of 20 Hz, is 150 data points large. It should be noted that the
buffers are larger than the actual time window of the training examples which is five
seconds long. The reason for this is that delays in the data transfer from the smartphone
to the central server using RabbitMQ could be observed. Hence, it is necessary to wait
until a sufficient amount of data is available to perform activity recognition. It was

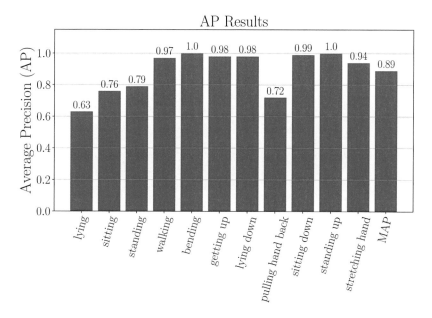

Figure 5.3: The average precision (AP) and mean average precision (MAP) are shown for all 11 activities.

already described in earlier sections that one criteria for a "sufficient" amount is to have enough subsequences to create a useful histogram for a specific activity. Hence, in the current system setup the length of the buffers can be defined very loosely using a rough estimation about the estimated time delay.

Finally, a real-time activity recognition is done every 2.5 seconds using the data that is stored in the buffers. However, it can be shown that the proposed system works much faster since the computational time for the feature extraction step from all available sensors and the recognition of the 11 activities only takes about 0.005 seconds and only 58MB of RAM. A demonstration video of the system can be found online[1]. The video shows that the system produces appropriate SVM scores as soon as the user performs an activity. In addition, the algorithm also tracks different changes of the user's posture. It should be noted that the activity system in the video does not incorporate smartglasses since it shows an older version of the system.

---

[1]https://youtu.be/sIL08IE_QLE

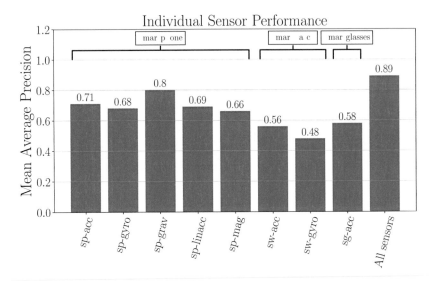

Figure 5.4: Comparison of the performance of individual sensors.

5.1.3 Effectiveness of Different Sensors and Devices

In the next paragraph the influence of each sensor on the performance of the activity recognition system is evaluated. The barplot in Fig. 5.4 summarises the achieved MAP results using all sensors individually. The rightmost bar in this figure shows the MAP of all sensors combined (88.8%). As can be depicted from Fig. 5.4, the gravity sensor of the smartphone has the best performance with a MAP of 80.0% when used alone. From a logical point of view, it is unclear why exactly this smartphone sensor delivers the highest individual performance of all 11 activities since hand and head movements typically cannot be tracked with a gravity sensor. Nevertheless, the movements should be important for the recognition of some of the activities. As an example, the activity "stretching hand" should be highly dependent on the measurement of hand movements, but the AP using only sp-grav results in a value of 77.3%. One explanation for this is that the sensor and the extracted features are able to recognise body movements that are characteristic for this activity, but are not part of the hand movement. In addition, it is important to see that the fusion of all sensors achieves the highest performance compared to using just a single sensor. This is a strong indicator that different sensors capture different characteristic parts of the activities and complement each other.

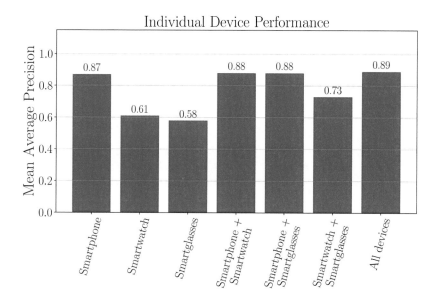

Figure 5.5: Comparison of the performance of individual devices.

One goal in the design of the system was to offer the user the possibility to turn sensors on and off whenever he/she feels that it is necessary or if certain situations arise (e.g. he/she forgets to wear the smartglasses). Following, these situations are simulated by evaluating only certain combinations of devices. In Fig. 5.5 the mean average precisions are shown that are obtained using the early fusion approach on sensors that are built into a single device, and combinations of these single devices. The last bar of Fig. 5.5 describes the overall result by combining all sensors, similar to the last bar in Fig. 5.3 and Fig. 5.4. From the results in Fig. 5.5 it is visible that using only the smartphone a MAP of 86.7% is achieved - almost the same score as the combination of all devices together. While this might lead to the conclusion that a smartphone alone can be enough to perform accurate activity recognition, the most probable explanation for this high performance is the current experimental setting in which only 11 basic activities are evaluated. Especially, only two of these activities can intuitively not be measured with a smartphone (hand activities). In future experiments more activities will be included to be able to monitor daily activities of users and it can be expected that the importance of smartwatch and smartglasses will therefore also increase. However, it

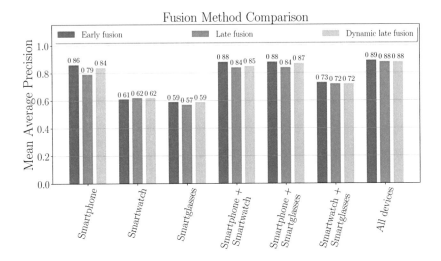

Figure 5.6: Comparison of the performance between early, late and dynamic late fusion.

should also be pointed out that the smartphone is the device with the broadest range of sensors. Given this fact, the author still expects that it will be the most influential device regarding the performance of activity recognition systems.

Finally, the barplot in Fig. 5.5 also indicates that the addition of new devices always improves the performance, and does not cause any performance degradation. Hence, given the proposed general framework it can be advised to add more devices if they are available.

5.1.4 Comparison of Different Fusion Approaches

In order to compare the performance of the early, late and dynamic late fusion approach different combinations of sensors are fused with each other using different fusion schemas. To obtain a statistically valid result, all possible combinations of devices and sensors were tried out. The result of the MAPs of different device combinations is shown in Fig. 5.6. Additionally, in total 255 different sensor combinations of the eight sensors were built to obtain all MAP values for these combinations. The results of this are presented in form of boxplots in Fig. 5.7. It can be seen that the various fusion approaches have comparable performances. This also includes that the dynamic late fusion approach in

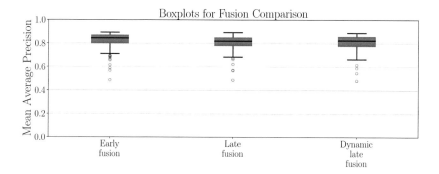

Figure 5.7: Boxplots for the different fusion approaches.

which weights are only calculated once for the usage of all sensors, can be an appropriate choice as a fusion schema and hence, helps saving computational effort.

5.1.5 Evaluation of Different Sampling Rates

Following, the effect of different sensor sampling rates on the performance of the activity recognition system is evaluated. It is of special interest how much the sampling rate can be reduced. With this knowledge the amount of data that needs to be transferred from the devices to the central server can be reduced to a minimum which consequently helps to prolong the battery life. For this evaluation five different scenarios for the sampling rate are chosen:

1. **Original:** The original case uses the fully available sampling rates that were also used in the previous experiments and where the MAP results in 88.8% as can be seen in the Figs. 5.3, 5.4, 5.5 and 5.6.

2. **Half of sampling rate:** All sensors' sampling rates are halved. Consequently, also the window size of the subsequences w_{sub} and the shifting parameter λ_{sub} are only half the size of the original. This results in $w_{\mathrm{sub}} = 64$ and $\lambda_{\mathrm{sub}} = 4$ for the sensors sp-acc, sp-gyro, sp-grav and sp-linacc, $w_{\mathrm{sub}} = 32$ and $\lambda_{\mathrm{sub}} = 2$ for the sensors sp-mag, sw-acc and sw-gyro and $w_{\mathrm{sub}} = 16$ and $\lambda_{\mathrm{sub}} = 1$ for the sg-acc sensor. The size of the codebook remains the same with a number of codewords of $N_\psi = 1024$.

3. **Half of codebook:** The sensor sampling rate of all sensors is also halved here which also results in the same parameters for w_{sub}, λ_{sub} and $N_\psi = 1024$ as in

	Original	Half SR	Half CB	Quarter SR	Quarter CB
Lying	0.63	0.67	0.61	0.73	0.56
Sitting	0.76	0.73	0.75	0.77	0.66
Standing	0.80	0.83	0.83	0.78	0.81
Walking	0.98	0.98	0.98	0.98	0.98
Bending	1.00	1.00	0.98	1.00	0.98
Getting up	0.98	1.00	1.00	0.99	0.99
Lying down	0.98	1.00	1.00	0.99	1.00
Pulling hand back	0.72	0.65	0.68	0.61	0.67
Sitting down	0.99	1.00	1.00	0.99	0.99
Standing up	1.00	1.00	1.00	1.00	1.00
Stretching hand	0.94	0.89	0.90	0.90	0.91
MAP	**0.88827**	**0.887584**	**0.884472**	**0.885211**	**0.867748**

Table 5.2: Overview of all results for the sampling rate evaluation.

the previous case. However, the codebooks are not re-calculated but instead the original codebooks are sub-sampled every second data point so that each codeword becomes half of its original size.

4. **Quarter of sampling rate:** Similar to the half-sampling-rate scenario, here the sampling rate is only one quarter of the original sampling rate. This leads to $w_{sub} = 32$ and $\lambda_{sub} = 2$ for sp-acc, sp-gyro, sp-grav and sp-linacc, $w_{sub} = 16$ and $\lambda_{sub} = 1$ for sp-mag, sw-acc and sw-gyro and $w_{sub} = 8$ and $\lambda_{sub} = 1$ for sg-acc.

5. **Quarter of a codebook:** This test scenario is the same like the half-codebook evaluation, but original codewords are sub-sampled every fourth data point.

Although it would be possible to exhaustively search for a set of parameters for each single sensor that would produce an overall best result, this methodology is not used in this evaluation since it would be contradictory to the claim of a general activity recognition framework. In addition, using only a quarter of the original sampling rate for the accelerometer of the smartglasses would result in a very low frequency of 5 Hz. Since it seems unreasonable to operate under such low sampling frequencies, this sensor was not used in this specific scenario. The results of the comparison are summarised in the barplot in the Fig. 5.8. The numerical results are given in table 5.2. It is clearly visible that the MAPs for all five sampling scenarios are very close to each other with values of 88.8%, 88.8%, 88.4%, 88.5% and 86.8%. These results show the general validity of the proposed framework in that it is capable to handle different sampling rates.

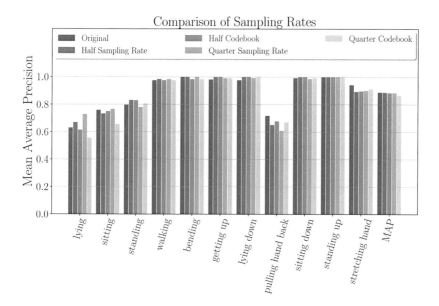

Figure 5.8: Performance comparison of different sampling rates. For each activity, the bars show from left to the right the original sampling rate, half of the sampling rate, half of the original codebook, a quarter of the sampling rate and a quarter of the original codebook.

Furthermore, the results suggest that most activities can already be reliably detected using very low sampling frequencies. This might change if a higher variety of more alike activities should be identified, but this must be tested with further experiments in the future. Only in rare cases the full sampling rate clearly dominates the reduced variants. Examples for this can be found for the two activities "pulling hand back" and "stretching hand". Since these are both hand-based activities, the smartwatch sensor with its already from the beginning low sampling frequency might have a higher influence here. With the down-sampled versions of the original codebooks it is possible to build solutions that dynamically adjust the sampling rate given some constraints, e.g. limited data transfer rate. Finally, since the experiments do not require the sensors to fulfil any prerequisites it can be expected that the system is able to work also on other sensors with varying sampling rates.

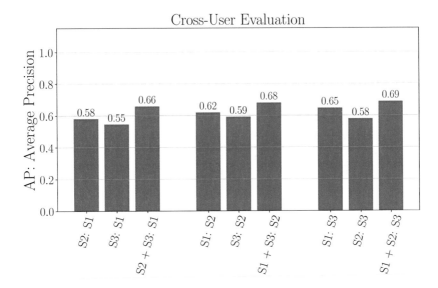

Figure 5.9: Overview of the results when performing cross-user evaluation. The bars show the obtained MAPs when the system was tested on the data of a user whose data is not part of the training dataset.

5.1.6   Cross-user Performance Examination

Next, the system's cross-user performance is evaluated by training the algorithm on the sensor data from one user and applying it to the data coming from other users. For this, the data from three different users $S1$, $S2$ and $S3$ is collected by the sensors sp-acc, sp-gyro, sp-grav, sp-linacc, sp-mag, sw-acc and sw-gyro. The smartglasses were not used within this test scenario. All 11 activities were performed at least 20 times by each user so that in total 264 activity executions were recorded for $S1$, 240 for $S2$ and 220 for $S3$. All parameters of the algorithm were set according to the previously described settings using the early fusion approach. Fig. 5.9 illustrates the MAPs obtained for the cross-user evaluation. Each bar in this plot shows the results when training the algorithm using one or two users and applying it to another user. More specific, the label of each bar denotes that the data of the user(s) left to the colon ":" are used for training while the user to the right of the colon was used for evaluation.

It can be seen that cross-user performances are in general worse than single-user performance described in earlier paragraphs. However, looking at the three groups in the plots, combining the training data of multiple users always leads to a higher score in comparison to just using a single user. This can be explained by the larger variety of training examples that is available during the training phase. Consequently, it can be expected that adding more training data to the training dataset will increase the performance even more. Nevertheless, this example also shows the high variation when executing different activities among different users which was introduced as one of the typical problems in the area of activity recognition. It can be concluded that solving this problem can be done in either of two ways: i) adding more training data from a high variety of different users to cover as many ways of executing an activity as possible ii) including some training examples that are specific to the user.

5.1.7 Comparison to the State of the Art

Finally, the proposed methodology will be tested on three different benchmark datasets. The first dataset was introduced by Picard et al. in [198] and has the goal to identify eight different emotions (e.g. anger, hate, joy, ...) using physiologic sensors like blood volume pressure, respiration rate, electrodermal activity and an electromyogram collected from a single person over the course of 20 days. This leads to in total 160 emotion instances where each sensor has a sampling rate of 20 Hz. The authors of this dataset perform activity recognition by extracting six statistical features like the mean, standard deviation and first-order derivatives for every sensor type and report an accuracy after leave-one-out cross validation of around 46.3%. The codebook method was evaluated on the same dataset and the same setting using 512 codewords, early fusion and soft assignment. With this an accuracy of 54.4% could be achieved.

The second dataset by Ofli et al. [185] evaluates the performance of activity recognition systems using six three-axis accelerometers attached to the user's body. In total 12 subjects perform 11 activities which results in 660 activity executions. The evaluation setup is similar to the aforementioned cross-user evaluation. The data of seven subjects is used within the training dataset while on five subjects the testing is performed. The proposed benchmark method of the authors uses a similar codebook approach. However, subsequences are only represented by its variance and only thirty subsequences are extracted. In contrast, the proposed codebook method performs on the dataset when using a dense sampling rate of $w_{sub} = 2$ and 512 codewords. This leads to an accuracy of 97.8% compared to 85.4% of the benchmark method.

The third and final dataset has been compiled by Bulling et al. [32]. In this dataset electrooculography (EOG) data was collected for typical office activities like reading a paper, taking a note or watching a video. The dataset consists of eight subjects that execute each activity twice. Along with this dataset the authors propose a new method to extract useful patterns from the eye movements. This includes a filtering step for

	Acc.		Acc.		Prec./Rec.
Codebook	54.4%	Codebook	97.8%	Codebook	66.9% / 61.3%
Picard et al.	46.3%	Ofli et al.	85.4%	Bulling et al.	76.1% / 70.5%

Table 5.3: Performance comparison on state of the art benchmark datasets. For the dataset of Picard and Ofli results are reported as the achieved accuracy, while for the dataset of Bulling the results reflect the precision and recall values.

preprocessing and finding typical eye movements like saccades, fixations and blinks. Each step requires several threshold and parameters that must be optimised. Nevertheless, this sophisticated method outperforms the codebook-based activity recognition by almost 10%. The precision and recall provided by Bulling reaches 76.1% and 70.5%, while the codebook approach results in 66.9% and 61.3%, respectively. All results are summarised in table 5.3.

5.2   Experimental Results for Indoor Localisation

The indoor localisation system is evaluated in a university building consisting of 4 floors where each floor has a size of 77 m × 55 m. For the data collection a Google Nexus 5 and a Samsung Galaxy S5 were used that contain all relevant sensors like an accelerometer and a gyroscope. As external information source the Wi-Fi signal of 5 access points was available. In addition six Bluetooth beacons were installed at selected places within the building. The Wi-Fi and Bluetooth beacons were calibrated with the required reference measurements at a given distance. Five different people walked a route of approximately 220 m throughout the building where each walk took around 5 minutes. The position of the user during his walk was collected by letting him click a button on the smartphone whenever he passed one of the pre-defined markers along the path. The path can be seen, for example, in Fig. 5.10 as black line. The path starts at the upper left corner and follows a straight path, then turning right and following a straight path again. After taking the stairs to the second floor, a 180° turn follows after which the user walks the stairs to the first floor and after short period of straight walking down the ground floor from which he returns back to start point using multiple staircases. All parameters within the statistical models were optimised using simple heuristics and trial-and-error and the relevant calculations were performed offline using 10000 particles.

Next, the results of different sensor combinations are presented in order to evaluate the influence of each sensor modality on the accuracy of the system. Hence, the same data was re-used for each single sensor combination. The first Fig. 5.10 illustrates a simple transition model in combination with a Wi-Fi information. The transition model

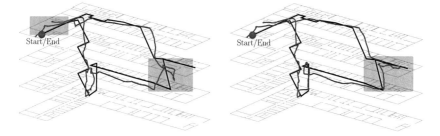

Figure 5.10: The image on the left shows the usage of only Wi-Fi with a simple transition model. The ground truth is given by a black line while the estimated position is drawn in blue. Both marked areas suffer from structural conditions of the building that negatively influence the Wi-Fi signal. On the right image additional beacons are used to stabilise the position estimation at this location.

estimates a new position based on the current position, but does not take any restrictions like walls into consideration. The estimated route, shown in blue colour in Fig. 5.10, clearly follows the ground truth path. This also includes all floor level changes. However, at some locations the Wi-Fi signal is disturbed due to structural conditions of the building. In addition, the low update rate of 4 seconds for the Wi-Fi signal sometimes leads to a significant loss of information, e.g. the 180° turn is only hardly recognised. Adding beacons to the some areas of the building decreased the median error from 6.48 m down to 4.97 m.

The improvement by changing from the simple transition model to the complex transition model is shown in Fig. 5.11. Here again Wi-Fi and beacons were used. It is visible from this image in comparison to Fig. 5.10 that the estimated path is much smoother and without strong outliers. Nevertheless, the path also depicts that especially floor level changes are often recognised late due to the sensor delay and consequently also because of the transition model. Since transition changes only occur along edges of the graph model and floor level changes only happen in regions where staircases are present, the transition model avoids these areas since it does not recognise a floor level change. Only a new sensor update that indicates a floor level change corrects this estimation with some time delay. To avoid these kind of situations a barometer with a higher sampling rate is introduced. While many situations can be resolved with the barometer sensor, still the long stairway towards the end of the path causes problems. This is mainly due to the assumption that a user is walking with constant speed, however, the walking speed on stairs is typically much lower. In addition, the transition model relies on a discrete representation of the floor levels while the pressure measured by the

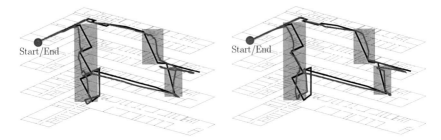

Figure 5.11: On the left side Wi-Fi and beacons are used together with the complex transition model. On the right image also barometer information is added. The boxes show situations in which a delay exists between the estimated and the real position. Adding barometer information with its higher sampling frequency helps to improve in these cases.

barometer changes smoothly. This again leads to estimation delays until the barometer displays a floor level change. Using the complex transition improved the deviation of the estimated path from the ground truth to 4.69 m on average and adding barometer information helped to reduce this further to 4.19 m.

On the left side of Fig. 5.12 the scenario is shown when only step and turn detection together with the barometer is used, but without any absolute position information. As usual for dead-reckoning approaches the position estimation at the beginning of the localisation is close to the ground truth, but deviates strongly after some time. In particular, it is not possible for the system to recover from a lost path without external information which leads to huge estimation errors. On the right side of Fig. 5.12 a situation is illustrated in which the user changes the orientation of the phone . While the red box marks the simple heading evaluation, the green box shows the heading model that utilises the von Mises distribution that "turns off" the sensor in order to avoid faulty measurements. The estimated path with this new evaluation is much smoother than with the old one which suffers from the confusing information.

Finally, all available sensors are used at the same time, so that in total Wi-Fi, beacons, barometer, step and turn information are included in the position estimation (see Fig. 5.13). Despite some areas that look worse compared to previous test scenarios, the overall accuracy reaches its best value with 3.75 m. This is especially given due to the decreased temporal delay between the estimation and the real path which is the result of additional sensors with higher sampling rate. Still, the most challenging locations are the staircases that cause most of the accumulated error. An overview of all results is given in table 5.4.

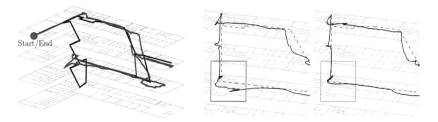

Figure 5.12: On the left side of the image the path is illustrated when only relative sensor information is used. After a short period of time the estimated path strongly deviates from the real path. The middle and right side show the effect of including the technique to exclude faulty gyroscope measurements when the user rotates his/her phone.

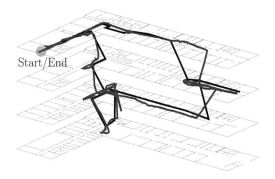

Figure 5.13: The resulting path when all available sensors are combined.

Transition	Wi-Fi	Beacons	Baro.	Step/Turn	$\tilde{\epsilon}$	$\bar{\epsilon}$	σ
Simple	✓				648	730	395
Simple	✓	✓			497	651	461
Graph	✓	✓			469	511	310
Graph	✓	✓	✓		419	459	294
Graph	✓	✓	✓	✓	376	416	201

Table 5.4: Overview of all results using different sensor combinations.

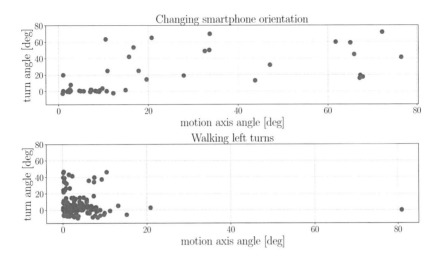

Figure 5.14: The top figure shows the case when the user changes the orientation of the phone. It is visible that whenever the gyroscope measures a change also changes of the motion axis are visible. Contrary, the bottom figure illustrates when the user walks multiple left turn while the orientation of the phone is relatively stable. Here changes of the motion axis show much smaller values compared to the top figure.

Fig. 5.14 shows two experiments regarding the estimation of the motion axis. Since the motion axis denotes the orientation of the smartphone in regard to the user, one can expect that changes of the smartphone orientation should also influence the motion axis estimation. This is tested by having a user holding a smartphone and turning it 90°, for example from landscape view to portrait view. The top image in Fig. 5.14 depicts the measurements that were taken during this experiment. The x-axis shows changes of the motion axis while the y-axis shows the measured heading change which is given by integrating over the gyroscope for 500 ms. It can be seen that for heading changes that are close to zero also the motion axis change is small but not completely zero. However, for larger heading changes also the motion axis changes are distributed over a wider range. This is in stark contrast to the bottom image of Fig. 5.14 where measurements were collected while a user made several left turns with the smarphone in a fixed position. Hence, values for the motion axis are much more in the lower range which indicates that the motion axis stayed mostly constant. With this knowledge it is possible to remove heading measurements whenever the motion axis shows large values

#Particles	Dead reckoning	Dead reckoning + User feedback	#Mediations
10000	57% (46/80)	67% (54/80)	21
50000	67% (54/80)	87% (70/80)	36

Table 5.5: The table summarises the results when user feedback is included into a simplistic localisation system.

with the proposed new heading approach. The effectiveness of this was illustrated in Fig. 5.12.

User feedback In order to test the performance of incorporating the user feedback into the system, a setup was chosen that only uses step and turn detection for localisation. With this it can be guaranteed that the following results are not influenced by external sources. A person walked 11 different routes through a university building whereby the starting position was known. In this case only room accuracy is of importance since it is not possible to get more details with the user feedback approach. Hence, the room provided by the system is compared with actual ground truth data and it is counted how often the correct room was estimated. Without the user feedback model the system could determine 46 out of 80 positions correctly which is equivalent to 57% accuracy utilising 10000 particles. Increasing the number of particles to 50000 resulted in an accuracy of 67%. Introducing the user feedback improved the results from 57% to 67% with 10000 particles and to 87% with 50000, respectively. The results are also shown in table 5.5. As seen, the user feedback can improve the accuracy significantly. However, the number of 21 and 36 mediations are rarely acceptable in an indoor localisation system since users are disturbed way too often. The high number of mediations origins in the low accuracy of the initial localisation system that only uses step and turn detection. With that, even if the current position is corrected by the user, it is still hard for the system to track the user's position since the heading information is never corrected. Furthermore, the experiments at hand always assumed the user to give a correct answer. While other cases could also be tested it would worsen the accuracy even more since less information is provided to the system.

Locomotion detection In Fig. 5.15 the results of the classification of different types of human locomotion are provided. In particular, the classes standing, walking, walking stairs up and stairs down, and driving with the elevator up and down should be distinguished. The final classification rate after a 6-fold-cross-validation was a precision of 95% and a recall of 94%. For the classification the time series signal was split into multiple overlapping windows with the goal to assign a label to each window. The results

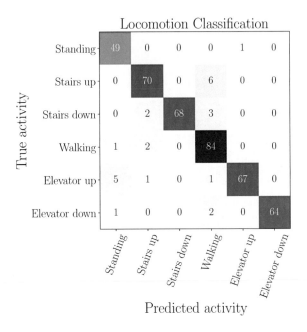

Figure 5.15: Confusion matrix for locomotion recognition.

were achieved by only utilising the accelerometer and barometer sensor. For this, only two features were needed - the magnitude of the variance of the accelerometer and the difference between the end and the beginning of the window for the barometer signal (see Chap. 2.3.2 for a detailed description).

An interesting observation could be made during the evaluation of the sensor data. The recording of the activities for the experiments was performed over two different days. Taking the mean of the barometer, it was already possible to distinguish among some activities. The reason for this lies in the different weather conditions on these days. Measuring just the barometer therefore was enough to separate among activities that were executed on different days which shows that one has to be careful when choosing features from sensors that measure environmental phenomena. An example for the activities sitting and walking stairs up is illustrated in Fig. 5.16.

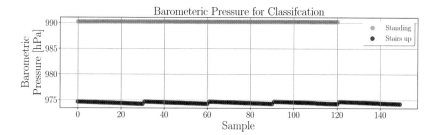

Figure 5.16: The example shows that the mean of the barometric pressure can already be an undesired classification feature.

5.3 Experimental Results for Gesture Recognition

The following section describes the experimental results that were achieved using the proposed gesture recognition system from Chap. 4.5.

5.3.1 MHAD dataset

The experiments were performed on the Multimodal Human Action Database (MHAD) dataset provided by [185]. Although this dataset was already used to evaluate the performance of the activity recognition system in the beginning section of this chapter, it can also be used as a gesture recognition benchmark. The reason for this is that most of the activities show a repetitive characteristic that could also be interpreted as whole-body gestures. Hence, it is a perfect test scenario to evaluate the performance of a multimodal approach for gesture recognition.

The original MHAD dataset consists of various sensor data ranging from RGB and Kinect cameras, audio sensors and accelerometers that are attached to the user's body (see Fig. 5.17). In total 12 different subjects (7 male and 5 female) perform 11 different activities which are 1. jumping in place, 2. jumping jacks, 3. bending, 4. punching, 5. waving with two hands, 6. waving with the right hand, 7. clapping hands, 8. throwing a ball with the right hand, 9. sitting down, then standing up, 10. sitting down and 11. standing up. Every activity was executed 5 times by every subject. Since the focus in this work lies on time series data, only the 6 accelerometers are utilised that are symmetrically attached to subjects' wrists, ankles and hips. Each accelerometer produces 3 time series - one for each axis - so that in total the data of 18 different sensors are available that are sampled with a frequency of 30 Hz.

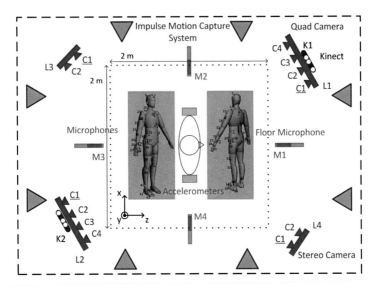

Figure 5.17: Overview of the sensors that are used within the Multimodal Human Action Database (MHAD) dataset [185]. Here, only the data of the accelerometers that are attached to the user's body are applied within the gesture recognition approach. Accelerometers are denotes as H1, H2, . . . , H6.

5.3.2   Experimental Results

The following results are obtained using the parameters $\mu = 1$ and $\sigma = 0.2$ for the normally distributed random variable α_k that is used within the state transition. The total number of particles is set to $N_{\Upsilon_t} = 120$, while after each resampling step 60 new particles are introduced to ensure a sufficient coverage of the probability space. Gestures are classified into a specific class if their probability exceeds the threshold value 0.7. With this setup an average accuracy of 85.30% can be reached across all gestures using a leave-one-out cross validation. The best result in this cross-validation could reach 91.90%, while the worst results was 72.73% with a standard deviation of 7.29%. A complete overview of the results is given in the confusion matrix in Fig. 5.18.

Taking a closer look at the confusion matrix, errors occur most often for gestures that include parts of other movements and therefore exhibit similar sensor values. This is especially true for the test cases "standing up", "sitting down" and the combination of "sitting down and standing up". In particular, for the latter one it can be seen in the confusion matrix that most confusions are due to the "sitting down" activity. However,

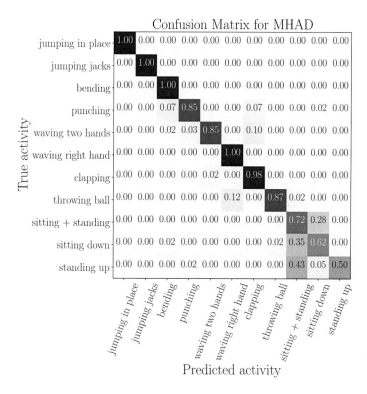

Figure 5.18: Confusion matrix for gesture recognition on MHAD dataset.

this is only a partial misclassification. The particle filter-based gesture recognition approach assigned the class label "sitting down" after a certain confidence threshold for this class was exceeded. However, it was not always able to identify that the gesture was not already finished but that a second part, the "sitting down" followed. So, in this case the method missed the second part of the gesture, but recognised the first part correctly. Contrary, for most of the other activities the algorithm achieves very high classification results, and, due to the training and testing schema, has also shown to work on user-independent tasks.

5.3.3   Comparison to the State of the Art

Next, the particle filter-based gesture recognition is tested against other state of the art techniques. These include:

- **Support Vector Machine:** The raw sensor data of all sensors is sliced into multiple windows and is used directly as input feature for the model. The window is shifted one data point to the right for each new window. The radial basis function (RBF) is chosen for the kernel as it known to be able to capture the structure of high-dimensional data.

- **Multi-Layer Perceptron:** The multi-layer perceptron (MLP) is a classical feed-forward neural network that is widely applied for many classification tasks. Equivalent to the SVM test case, data is again split into multiple windows.

- **Convolutional Neural Network:** Convolutional neural networks (CNN) are typically deep neural networks that extract features by applying a convolution on the raw input data. The CNN applied here consists of two pairs of convolutional and pooling layers. The final classification is executed by an MLP at the end of the CNN using the automatically extracted features. The network is trained using a mini-batch gradient descent.

The three classification methods have been trained using leaving one out cross validation using the data from all 12 subjects. The hyper-parameters were optimised using a grid search. With this, the following results could be achieved that are summarised in table 5.6. The proposed particle filter method achieves a higher accuracy than all of

Accuracy	Average	Max	Min	Std
Particle filter	85.30%	91.83%	72.73%	7.29%
SVM	75.52%	88.95%	14.58%	19.79%
MLP	79.22%	90.57%	61.93%	7.41%
CNN	79.56%	90.84%	61.94%	7.99%

Table 5.6: Comparison of particle filter method with state of the art methods.

the compared methods averaged over the 12 folds of the cross validation. The method also comes with the advantage of not having to specify a shift-parameter for the input windows. The performance of the neural networks and the SVM especially suffers from some low performance for specific subjects. For the SVM this can be explained by using just the raw data as an input which probably does not contain enough relevant information for an appropriate classification. On the other hand, the MHAD dataset might not be large and diverse enough for (deep) neural network approaches which limits their capability of efficiently learning useful structures in the data. One can expect that applying feature extraction or more sophisticated methods will achieve higher classification results. This was shown at the beginning of the chapter, where the codebook approach resulted in a classification rate of 97.8%. Nevertheless, the benchmark method of Ofli [185] performed with 85.4% only slightly better than the particle filter approach which indicates the potential of this method.

Chapter 6

Conclusion

The chapter closes this theses by giving a short overview of the addressed problems. In particular, the codebook-based method for activity and the state estimation framework for indoor localisation are reviewed. Finally, a list of points is provided to further improve the proposed solutions in the future.

6.1   Summary

The fusion of the output of multiple sensors is an important source to generate information that is not available if a single sensor alone would monitor the scene. Especially today, many everyday devices like smartphones and smartwatches are equipped with many sensors. In this thesis the focus lies on the sensors that are provided within these devices. In particular, this includes accelerometer, gyroscopes, magnetometers, barometers and gravity sensors, but also physical sensors like heart-rate and electrodermal activity sensors. The benefit of fusing these kinds of sensors was presented in three use cases.

Feature learning in activity recognition   In the field of activity recognition the goal is to identify the activity that a person is currently performing. With this information new applications in the area of elderly care and self-quantisation are possible. Activity recognition is a typical example for a classification problem. The aim is to assign a certain period of time to one of multiple pre-defined activities. For this the aforementioned sensors are available that track the person's movement. In the classical pattern recognition pipeline the raw sensor data is transformed into features which are a compact representation of characteristic properties of the data. However, traditionally this feature extraction step is a manual task that requires a significant amount of domain knowledge and creativity to come up with a good feature representation. The current trend in the area of machine learning is to automatise the feature extraction step by so called feature learning methods. Here, especially deep neural networks play an important role and are currently the state of the art. While neural networks are successfully applied in many domains like image and speech recognition, coming up with an appropriate architecture and tuning the multitude of parameters often is a tedious task that relies a lot on intuition an experience. The codebook-based method proposed in this thesis can also be considered as a feature learning method, but gets by with only a few intuitive parameters. The basic idea is similar to the bag-of-words approach from text classification and bag-of-visual-words approach from image recognition, but is here applied to time series data. Based on an unlabelled dataset a codebook is constructed that contains different subsequences which are short parts of the time series. Subsequences are clustered into codewords, where each codeword represents a characteristic part of the time series. Following, each sequence that should be classified can be transformed into a new representation by counting how often specific subsequences occur within the sequence. Similar activities are supposed to have a similar distribution of codewords. Using this approach a general framework for activity recognition was presented. In this framework multiple sensors are transferring the data with a messaging protocol to a central server where the activity recognition takes place. Since the codebook-based classifier that does not require any specific domain knowledge or preprocessing, the framework can be extended easily by new sensors. The codebook approach was successfully tested on a dataset consisting of 11 basic activities. In addition a comparison was conduced with multiple state of the art benchmark datasets from the fields of activity and emotion recognition.

State estimation in indoor localisation   The second part of the thesis considered the problem of state estimation. Here, the problem is to estimate the state $\mathbf{q}$ that is not directly observable with any sensor. Instead sensors provide measurements that are indirectly related to the hidden variable. A popular technique for these kind of problems is recursive state estimation which derives a probability density over the hidden state space and is based on Bayes' rule. Within the recursive state estimation framework two statistical models must be defined. The state transition statistically models the probability of how the state evolves over time. To encounter the noise of the sensor measurements an observation relates the sensor measurement to the hidden variable in a probabilistic manner. While the state transition model adds uncertainty to the estimated probability density, the observation model adds new information to counteract the introduced uncertainty. This framework was applied to the problem of indoor localisation. The aim in indoor localisation is to estimate the position of user within a building. While this is a solved problem in the outdoor area using satellite based navigation systems, the signals of these systems are usually not receivable within buildings. Hence, the position of a user is considered to be hidden, but sensor measurements like the acceleration during his/her walking phases and the constantly received signal strength from Wi-Fi access points deliver enough information to infer and track his/her position. Within this work a complete indoor localisation was proposed fusing the data of multiple sensors. The main contributions of this work are the statistical models that are related to the pedestrians walking behaviour. In particular, step information was included into the transition model as a Gaussian mixture distribution to distinguish among cases of walking and standing. The recognition of different locomotion modes of the user were introduced as activity recognition task. As additional component the gyroscope was used as an indicator for the user's walking direction. A mechanism was proposed to cope with measurements that are potentially erroneous. For this the user's motion axis was related to the von Mises distribution. Whenever a significant deviation of the motion axis is recognised the confidence into the corresponding gyroscope values is reduced. Finally, the user's feedback was introduced as additional information source. Experiments within a large-scale building showed that the system is able to track a user over multiple floor levels with average accuracies of about 3.7 m.

State estimation and classification in gesture recognition Finally, the recursive state estimation framework was applied to the problem of gesture recognition. The main challenges in gesture recognition are the identification of gestures without an explicit signal, the fast detection of gestures to allow a smooth user experience and various executions of the same gesture. Recursive state estimation, in particular particle filtering, was chosen for this problem since it delivers a probability density for the hidden state space for each point in time. In contrast, many other gesture recognition methods have to wait for a certain amount of time until enough data was collected for the specific time window. By modelling the gesture recognition problem similar to a localisation problem it could be shown that many whole-body gestures could successfully be identified with high accuracy. For this, the class label as discrete variable and the point in time of the gesture was included into the hidden state. During the training phase an average gesture was calculated using a training dataset of multiple users across a variety of sensors. For the calculation of the average gesture Dynamic Time Warping Barycentric Averaging (DBA) was utilised which averages multiple time series by using the distance matrix provided by Dynamic Time Warping. Since the outputs of this algorithm are without timestamp, an additional conversion step was introduced that is able to relate real-time sensor data to the averaged gesture templates.

6.2   Future Work

The proposed approaches have been successfully applied in various applications and have shown to be competitive with state of the art methods. However, there is still room for further improvement:

Transfer Learning   One of the biggest challenges in activity recognition is the laborious task of collecting labelled data. So, it is even more important to make optimal use of the available data. One technique that has gained popularity in the recent history is transfer learning [189]. The main idea of transfer learning is to adapt the knowledge from a source domain where a lot of data is available to a target domain where none or only very little data exists. Since one prerequisite in machine learning is that the training data and the test data have a common feature space and follow the same probability distribution, the special challenge in transfer learning lies in an appropriate transformation from the original domain to the new target domain. Hence, several ways were proposed in which the transfer of knowledge from one domain to another domain can happen. Instance transfer tries to reuse examples from the source domain in the target domain [51]. In the field of activity recognition this idea could be applied for the development of user-independent systems. Training data collected for a specific user can be adopted to the unlabelled data of unknown users. Another possibility to reuse existing knowledge is to transfer the feature representation of the source domain to the target domain. An example for this is the adoption of one sensor modality to a new modality. For example, [107] transfer the feature spaces and labels from a known source to an unlabelled target domain. In general, feature representations can be transferred by a transfer function that is learned from the data or by manually identifying such a function. Another approach is to find a common feature space in which both, source and target data, can be fitted to. Finally, the third possibility of transfer learning is to carry over hyper-parameters of the learning algorithm. As shown by [236] the parameters of a Hidden Markov Model were learned on the basis of the source data and unlabelled data from the target domain.

Besides activity recognition, transfer learning could also be successfully applied in the field of indoor localisation. In Wi-Fi localisation received signal strengths of the Wi-Fi measurements can be transferred over a period of time if environmental changes have taken place and changed the initially collected signal map [190].

Different codebook encoding   In the codebook-based activity recognition method, the distribution of codewords within a sequence of data is represented as a histogram using an hard-assignment or soft-assignment approach. However, there are several alternatives to this encoding [38]. For example, Fisher vector encoding captures various statistical properties like the distance of the local descriptors from its assigned code-word and the distance to all other codewords. For this, the K-means clustering step is exchanged by a Gaussian mixture model. In this work local descriptors were the subsequences of the time series data. However, statistical features extracted from the data like the mean and variance of the subsequences can also be added. The result of this encoding is a high-dimensional vector which has been successfully combined with linear classifiers [193] in image classification. Further possible encodings to test are the super vector encoding [265] or locality-constrained linear encodings [244].

All these different encodings can potentially enhance the existing feature represen-tation, leading to higher accuracies and allowing to apply faster learning methods like the linear version of a SVM version.

Extension to complex activities Given the current experiments for activity recog-nition, very basic activities like sitting or walking were determined. In the future the aim is to use these *atomic* activities as building blocks for more complex activities, e.g. cooking, doing sports or shopping. Since such complex activities can be represented as a multitude of atomic activities, in principal a similar histogram-based activity recogni-tion approach can be chosen. However, instead of counting the occurrence of time series subsequences, an activity should be identifiable using a histogram of atomic activities. With this, a hierarchy of more and more complex activities can be built, where each complex activity is represented as a set of less complex activities. In order to test such an approach, it is necessary to train the current system on a higher variety of very basic activities and to build up a "vocabulary of activities".

Combining indoor localisation and activity recognition Several papers have already pointed out that the knowledge of the user's current location is an important source of information for the recognition of activities. Especially within private apart-ments the position often can only be tracked by installing additional sensors like beacons or other forms of proximity sensors. Employing the output of the proposed localisation system could further improve the accuracy of the activity recognition while at the same time no additional hardware besides the wearable devices would be needed. For this to work, statistical models like the transition model have to be adopted to the scenario of an apartment. The walking behaviour, for example, will be quite different within an apartment compared to a large-scale building like a mall or university building. An addi-tional, and much more fine-grained step detection together with a step length estimation are necessary to capture these different requirements.

Bibliography

[1]   G. D. Abowd, A. F. Bobick, I. A. Essa, E. D. Mynatt, and W. A. Rogers. 'The Aware Home: A Living Laboratory for Technologies For Successful Aging'. In: *Proceedings of the AAAI-02 Workshop: Automation as Caregiver*. 2002, pp. 1–7.

[2]   G. D. Abowd, A. K. Dey, P. J. Brown, N. Davies, M. Smith, and P. Steggles. 'Towards a Better Understanding of Context and Context-Awareness'. In: *Proceedings of the 1st International Symposium on Handheld and Ubiquitous Computing*. 1999, pp. 304–307.

[3]   U. R. Acharya, H. Fujita, V. K. Sudarshan, S. Bhat, and J. E. Koh. 'Application of Entropies For Automated Diagnosis of Epilepsy Using EEG Signals: A Review'. In: *Knowledge-Based Systems* 88.C (2015), pp. 85–96.

[4]   U. R. Acharya, H. Fujita, M. Adam, O. S. Lih, V. K. Sudarshan, T. J. Hong, J. E. Koh, Y. Hagiwara, C. K. Chua, C. K. Poo, and T. R. San. 'Automated Characterization and Classification of Coronary Artery Disease and Myocardial Infarction by Decomposition of ECG Signals: A Comparative Study'. In: *Information Sciences* 377 (2017), pp. 17–29.

[5]   M. Addlesee, R. Curwen, S. Hodges, J. Newman, P. Steggles, A. Ward, and A. Hopper. 'Implementing a Sentient Computing System'. In: *IEEE Computer* 34.8 (2001), pp. 50–56.

[6]   R. Agrawal, C. Faloutsos, and A. Swami. 'Efficient Similarity Search in Sequence Databases'. In: *Foundations of Data Organization and Algorithms*. 1993, pp. 69–84.

[7]   A. Akl, C. Feng, and S. Valaee. 'A Novel Accelerometer-Based Gesture Recognition System'. In: *IEEE Transactions on Signal Processing* 59.12 (2011), pp. 6197–6205.

[8]   C. Andrieu, N. de Freitas, A. Doucet, and M. I. Jordan. 'An Introduction to MCMC for Machine Learning'. In: *Machine Learning* 50.1 (2003), pp. 5–43.

[9]   M. S. Arulampalam, S. Maskell, N. Gordon, and T. Clapp. 'A Tutorial on Particle Filters for Online Nonlinear/Non-Gaussian Bayesian Tracking'. In: *IEEE Transactions on Signal Processing* 50.2 (2002), pp. 174–188.

[10] L. Atallah, B. Lo, R. King, and G. Z. Yang. 'Sensor Positioning for Activity Recognition Using Wearable Accelerometers'. In: *IEEE Transactions on Biomedical Circuits and Systems* 5.4 (2011), pp. 320–329.

[11] A. W. S. Au, C. Feng, S. Valaee, S. Reyes, S. Sorour, S. N. Markowitz, D. Gold, K. Gordon, and M. Eizenman. 'Indoor Tracking and Navigation Using Received Signal Strength and Compressive Sensing on a Mobile Device'. In: *IEEE Transactions on Mobile Computing* 12.10 (2013), pp. 2050–2062.

[12] A. Bagnall, L. Davis, J. Hills, and J. Lines. 'Transformation Based Ensembles for Time Series Classification'. In: *Proceedings of the 12th SIAM International Conference on Data Mining.* 2012, pp. 307–319.

[13] A. Bagnall, J. Lines, A. Bostrom, J. Large, and E. Keogh. 'The Great Time Series Classification Bake Off: A Review and Experimental Evaluation of Recent Algorithmic Advances'. In: *Data Mining and Knowledge Discovery* 31.3 (2017), pp. 606–660.

[14] P. Bahl and V. N. Padmanabhan. 'RADAR: An In-building RF-based User Location and Tracking System'. In: *Proceedings of the 19h Annual Joint Conference of the IEEE Computer and Communications Societies.* 2000, 775–784 vol.2.

[15] J. M. Baker, L. Deng, J. Glass, S. Khudanpur, C. h. Lee, N. Morgan, and D. O'Shaughnessy. 'Developments and Directions in Speech Recognition and Understanding, Part 1'. In: *IEEE Signal Processing Magazine* 26.3 (2009), pp. 75–80.

[16] J. Bakker, M. Pechenizkiy, and N. Sidorova. 'What's Your Current Stress Level? Detection of Stress Patterns from GSR Sensor Data'. In: *Proceedings of the 11th IEEE International Conference on Data Mining Workshops.* 2011, pp. 573–580.

[17] O. Banos, R. Garcia, J. Holgado-Terriza, M. Damas, H. Pomares, I. Rojas, A. Saez, and C. Villalonga. 'mHealthDroid: A Novel Framework for Agile Development of Mobile Health Applications'. In: *Proceedings of the International Workshop on Ambient Assisted Living: Ambient Assisted Living and Daily Activities.* 2014, pp. 91–98.

[18] O. Banos, M. A. Toth, M. Damas, H. Pomares, and I. Rojas. 'Dealing With the Effects of Sensor Displacement in Wearable Activity Recognition'. In: *Sensors* 14.6 (2014), pp. 9995–10023.

[19] O. Banos, M. A. Toth, M. Damas, H. Pomares, and I. Rojas. 'Dealing with the Effects of Sensor Displacement in Wearable Activity Recognition'. In: *Sensors* 14.6 (2014), pp. 9995–10023.

[20] P. Barralon, N. Vuillerme, and N. Noury. 'Walk Detection With a Kinematic Sensor: Frequency and Wavelet Comparison'. In: *Proceedings of the International Conference of the IEEE Engineering in Medicine and Biology Society.* 2006, pp. 1711–1714.

[21] M. G. Baydogan, G. Runger, and E. Tuv. 'A Bag-of-Features Framework to Classify Time Series'. In: *IEEE Transactions on Pattern Analysis and Machine Intelligence* 35.11 (2013), pp. 2796–2802.

[22] M. Benedek and C. Kaernbach. 'A Continuous Measure of Phasic Electrodermal Activity'. In: *Journal of Neuroscience Methods* 190.1 (2010), pp. 80–91.

[23] Y. Bengio, A. Courville, and P. Vincent. 'Representation Learning: A Review and New Perspectives'. In: *IEEE Transactions on Pattern Analysis and Machine Intelligence* 35.8 (2013), pp. 1798–1828.

[24] Y. Bengio. 'Practical Recommendations for Gradient-Based Training of Deep Architectures'. In: *Neural Networks: Tricks of the Trade: Second Edition.* Ed. by G. Montavon, G. B. Orr, and K.-R. Müller. Berlin, Heidelberg: Springer, 2012, pp. 437–478.

[25] D. J. Berndt and J. Clifford. 'Using Dynamic Time Warping to Find Patterns in Time Series'. In: *Proceedings of the 3rd International Conference on Knowledge Discovery and Data Mining.* 1994, pp. 359–370.

[26] E. Bhasker, S. Brown, and W. G. Griswold. 'Employing User Feedback for Fast, Accurate, Low-maintenance Geolocationing'. In: *Proceedings of the 2nd IEEE Annual Conference on Pervasive Computing and Communications.* 2004, pp. 111–120.

[27] C. M. Bishop. *Pattern Recognition and Machine Learning (Information Science and Statistics).* Secaucus, NJ, USA: Springer-Verlag New York, Inc., 2006. ISBN: 0387310738.

[28] M. J. Black and A. D. Jepson. 'A Probabilistic Framework for Matching Temporal Trajectories: Condensation-based Recognition of Gestures and Expressions'. In: *Proceedings of the 5th European Conference on Computer Vision Proceedings, Volume I.* 1998, pp. 909–924.

[29] P. Blanchart, L. He, and F. Le Gland. 'Information Fusion for Indoor Localization'. In: *Proceedings of the 12th International Conference on Information Fusion.* 2009, pp. 2083–2090.

[30] P. Bolliger. 'Redpin - Adaptive, Zero-configuration Indoor Localization Through User Collaboration'. In: *Proceedings of the 1st ACM International Workshop on Mobile Entity Localization and Tracking in GPS-less Environments*. 2008, pp. 55–60.

[31] M. Brunato and R. Battiti. 'Statistical Learning Theory for Location Fingerprinting in Wireless LANs'. In: *Computer Networks* 47.6 (2005), pp. 825–845.

[32] A. Bulling, J. Ward, H. Gellersen, and G. Tröster. 'Eye Movement Analysis for Activity Recognition Using Electrooculography'. In: *IEEE Transactions on Pattern Analysis and Machine Intelligence* 33.4 (2011), pp. 741–753.

[33] A. Bulling, U. Blanke, and B. Schiele. 'A Tutorial on Human Activity Recognition Using Body-worn Inertial Sensors'. In: *ACM Computing Surveys* 46.3 (2014), 33:1–33:33.

[34] A. Calatroni, D. Roggen, and G. Tröster. 'Collection and Curation of a Large Reference Dataset for Activity Recognition'. In: *Proceedings of the IEEE International Conference on Systems, Man, and Cybernetics*. 2011, pp. 30–35.

[35] O. Cappe, S. J. Godsill, and E. Moulines. 'An Overview of Existing Methods and Recent Advances in Sequential Monte Carlo'. In: *Proceedings of the IEEE* 95.5 (2007), pp. 899–924.

[36] B. Caramiaux, N. Montecchio, A. Tanaka, and F. Bevilacqua. 'Adaptive Gesture Recognition with Variation Estimation for Interactive Systems'. In: *ACM Transactions on Interactive Intelligent Systems* 4.4 (2014), 18:1–18:34.

[37] C.-C. Chang and C.-J. Lin. 'LIBSVM: A Library for Support Vector Machines'. In: *ACM Transactions on Intelligent Systems and Technology* 2.3 (2011), 27:1–27:27.

[38] K. Chatfield, V. Lempitsky, A. Vedaldi, and A. Zisserman. 'The Devil Is in the Details: An Evaluation of Recent Feature Encoding Methods'. In: *Proceedings of the British Machine Vision Conference*. 2011, pp. 76.1–76.12.

[39] R. Chavarriaga, H. Sagha, A. Calatroni, S. T. Digumarti, G. Tröster, J. del R. Millán, and D. Roggen. 'The Opportunity challenge: A benchmark database for on-body sensor-based activity recognition'. In: *Pattern Recognition Letters* 34.15 (2013), pp. 2033–2042.

[40] S. S. Chawathe. 'Low-Latency Indoor Localization Using Bluetooth Beacons'. In: *Proceedings of the 12th International IEEE Conference on Intelligent Transportation Systems*. 2009, pp. 1–7.

[41] F. Chen, P. Deng, J. Wan, D. Zhang, A. V. Vasilakos, and X. Rong. 'Data Mining for the Internet of Things: Literature Review and Challenges'. In: *International Journal of Distributed Sensor Networks* 11.8 (2015), pp. 1–14.

[42] L. Chen, J. Hoey, C. D. Nugent, D. J. Cook, and Z. Yu. 'Sensor-based Activity Recognition'. In: *IEEE Transactions on Systems, Man, and Cybernetics, Part C (Applications and Reviews)* 42.6 (2012), pp. 790–808.

[43] Z. Chen, Q. Zhu, and Y. C. Soh. 'Smartphone Inertial Sensor-based Indoor Localization and Tracking With iBeacon Corrections'. In: *IEEE Transactions on Industrial Informatics* 12.4 (2016), pp. 1540–1549.

[44] Z. Chen. 'Bayesian Filtering: From Kalman Filters to Particle Filters, and Beyond'. In: *Statistics* 182.1 (2003), pp. 1–69.

[45] Z. Chen, H. Zou, H. Jiang, Q. Zhu, Y. C. Soh, and L. Xie. 'Fusion of WiFi, Smartphone Sensors and Landmarks Using the Kalman Filter for Indoor Localization'. In: *Sensors* 15.1 (2015), pp. 715–732.

[46] K. Chintalapudi, A. Padmanabha Iyer, and V. N. Padmanabhan. 'Indoor Localization Without the Pain'. In: *Proceedings of the 16th Annual International Conference on Mobile Computing and Networking.* 2010, pp. 173–184.

[47] H. S. Chudgar, S. Mukherjee, and K. Sharma. 'S Control: Accelerometer-based Gesture Recognition for Media Control'. In: *Proceedings of the International Conference on Advances in Electronics, Computers and Communications.* 2014, pp. 1–6.

[48] J. Chung, M. Donahoe, C. Schmandt, I.-J. Kim, P. Razavai, and M. Wiseman. 'Indoor Location Sensing Using Geo-magnetism'. In: *Proceedings of the 9th International Conference on Mobile Systems, Applications, and Services.* 2011, pp. 141–154.

[49] I. Cleland, B. Kikhia, C. Nugent, A. Boytsov, J. Hallberg, K. Synnes, S. McClean, and D. Finlay. 'Optimal Placement of Accelerometers for the Detection of Everyday Activities'. In: *Sensors* 13.7 (2013), pp. 9183–9200.

[50] A. Coates and A. Y. Ng. 'Learning Feature Representations with K-Means'. In: *Neural Networks: Tricks of the Trade: Second Edition.* Ed. by G. Montavon, G. B. Orr, and K.-R. Müller. Berlin, Heidelberg: Springer, 2012, pp. 561–580.

[51] D. J. Cook, A. S. Crandall, B. L. Thomas, and N. C. Krishnan. 'CASAS: A Smart Home in a Box'. In: *Computer* 46.7 (2013), pp. 62–69.

[52] A. Corradini. 'Dynamic Time Warping for Off-line Recognition of a Small Gesture Vocabulary'. In: *Proceedings of the IEEE ICCV Workshop on Recognition, Analysis, and Tracking of Faces and Gestures in Real-Time Systems*. 2001, pp. 82–89.

[53] G. Csurka, C. Dance, L. Fan, J. Willamowski, and C. Bray. 'Visual Categorization with Bags of Keypoints'. In: *Proceedings of the Workshop on Statistical Learning in Computer Vision*. 2004, pp. 1–22.

[54] P. K. Dash, M. Nayak, M. R. Senapati, and I. W. C. Lee. 'Mining for Similarities in Time Series Data Using Wavelet-based Feature Vectors and Neural Networks'. In: *Engineering Applications of Artificial Intelligence*. 20.2 (2007), pp. 185–201.

[55] N. de Freitas, C. Andrieu, P. Højen-Sørensen, M. Niranjan, and A. Gee. 'Sequential Monte Carlo Methods in Practice'. In: ed. by A. Doucet, N. de Freitas, and N. Gordon. New York: Springer, 2001. Chap. Sequential Monte Carlo Methods for Neural Networks.

[56] F. Deinzer, C. Derichs, and H. Niemann. 'A Framework for Actively Selecting Viewpoints in Object Recognition'. In: *International Journal of Pattern Recognition and Artificial Intelligence* 23.4 (2009), pp. 765–799.

[57] F. Dellaert, W. Burgard, D. Fox, and S. Thrun. 'Using the CONDENSATION Algorithm for Robust, Vision-based Mobile Robot Localization'. In: *Proceedings of the IEEE Computer Society Conference on Computer Vision and Pattern Recognition*. 1999, pp. 588–594.

[58] A. K. Dey and J. Mankoff. 'Designing Mediation for Context-aware Applications'. In: *ACM Transactions on Computer-Human Interaction* 12.1 (2005), pp. 53–80.

[59] J. J. M. Diaz, R. d. A. Maués, R. B. Soares, E. F. Nakamura, and C. M. S. Figueiredo. 'Bluepass: An Indoor Bluetooth-based Localization System for Mobile Applications'. In: *Proceedings of the IEEE Symposium on Computers and Communications*. 2010, pp. 778–783.

[60] A. Doucet, N. de Freitas, and N. Gordon. 'Sequential Monte Carlo Methods in Practice'. In: ed. by A. Doucet, N. de Freitas, and N. Gordon. New York: Springer, 2001. Chap. An Introduction to Sequential Monte Carlo Methods.

[61] A. Doucet, S. Godsill, and C. Andrieu. 'On Sequential Monte Carlo Sampling Methods for Bayesian Filtering'. In: *Statistics and Computing* 10.3 (2000), pp. 197–208.

[62] A. Doucet and A. M. Johansen. 'A Tutorial on Particle Filtering and Smoothing: Fifteen years later'. In: *The Oxford Handbook of Nonlinear Filtering*. Ed. by D. Crisan and B. Rozovsky. Oxford University Press, 2011.

[63] R. O. Duda, P. E. Hart, and D. G. Stork. *Pattern Classification*. 2nd Edition. New York, NY, USA: Wiley-Interscience, 2000.

[64] F. Ebner, T. Fetzer, F. Deinzer, and M. Grzegorzek. 'On Prior Navigation Knowledge in Multi Sensor Indoor Localisation'. In: *Proceedings of the 19th International Conference on Information Fusion*. 2016, pp. 557–564.

[65] F. Ebner, T. Fetzer, L. Köping, M. Grzegorzek, and F. Deinzer. 'Multi Sensor 3D Indoor Localisation'. In: *Indoor Positioning and Indoor Navigation (IPIN 2015), 2015 International Conference on*. Oct. 2015, pp. 1–11.

[66] F. Ebner, L. Köping, M. Grzegorzek, and F. Deinzer. 'Robust Self-Localization Using WiFi, Step/Turn-Detection and Recursive Density Estimation'. In: *Proceedings of the 5th International Conference on Indoor Positioning and Indoor Navigation*. 2014.

[67] V. Erceg, L. J. Greenstein, S. Y. Tjandra, S. R. Parkoff, A. Gupta, B. Kulic, A. A. Julius, and R. Bianchi. 'An Empirically Based Path Loss Model for Wireless Channels in Suburban Environments'. In: *IEEE Journal on Selected Areas in Communications* 17.7 (1999), pp. 1205–1211.

[68] M. O. Ernst and H. H. Bülthoff. 'Merging the Senses Into a Robust Percept'. In: *Trends in Cognitive Sciences* 8.4 (2004), pp. 162–169.

[69] F. Evennou, F. Marx, and E. Novakov. 'Map-aided Indoor Mobile Positioning System Using Particle Filter'. In: *Proceedings of the IEEE Wireless Communications and Networking Conference*. Vol. 4. 2005, pp. 2490–2494.

[70] T. Fetzer, F. Deinzer, L. Köping, and M. Grzegorzek. 'Statistical Indoor Localization Using Fusion of Depth-images and Step Setection'. In: *Proceedings of the International Conference on Indoor Positioning and Indoor Navigation*. 2014, pp. 407–415.

[71] T. Fetzer, F. Ebner, F. Deinzer, L. Köping, and M. Grzegorzek. 'On Monte Carlo Smoothing in Multi Sensor Indoor Localisation'. In: *Proceedings of the International Conference on Indoor Positioning and Indoor Navigation*. 2016, pp. 1–8.

[72] G. Forestier, F. Lalys, L. Riffaud, B. Trelhu, and P. Jannin. 'Classification of Surgical Processes Using Dynamic Time Warping'. In: *Journal of Biomedical Informatics* 45.2 (2012), pp. 255–264.

[73] D. Fox, J. Hightower, L. Liao, D. Schulz, and G. Borriello. 'Bayesian Filtering for Location Estimation'. In: *Pervasive Computing, IEEE* 2.3 (2003), pp. 24–33.

[74] E. Foxlin. 'Pedestrian Tracking with Shoe-mounted Inertial Sensors'. In: *IEEE Computer Graphics and Applications* 25.6 (2005), pp. 38–46.

[75] H. T. Friis. 'A Note on a Simple Transmission Formula'. In: *Proceedings of the IRE* 34.5 (1946), pp. 254–256.

[76] T.-c. Fu. 'A Review on Time Series Data Mining'. In: *Engineering Applications of Artificial Intelligence* 24.1 (2011), pp. 164–181.

[77] Y. Fukuju, M. Minami, H. Morikawa, and T. Aoyama. 'DOLPHIN: An Autonomous Indoor Positioning System in Ubiquitous Computing Environment'. In: *Proceedings of the IEEE Workshop on Software Technologies for Future Embedded Systems.* 2003, pp. 53–56.

[78] B. D. Fulcher and N. S. Jones. 'Highly Comparative Feature-Based Time-Series Classification'. In: *IEEE Transactions on Knowledge and Data Engineering* 26.12 (Dec. 2014), pp. 3026–3037.

[79] B. D. Fulcher, M. A. Little, and N. S. Jones. 'Highly Comparative Time Series Analysis: The Empirical Structure of Time Series and Their Methods'. In: *Journal of The Royal Society Interface* 10.83 (2013).

[80] M. Garbarino, M. Lai, D. Bender, R. W. Picard, and S. Tognetti. 'Empatica E3 . A Wearable Wireless Multi-sensor Device For Real-time Computerized Biofeedback and Data Acquisition'. In: *Proceedings of the 4th International Conference on Wireless Mobile Communication and Healthcare - Transforming Healthcare Through Innovations in Mobile and Wireless Technologies.* 2014, pp. 39–42.

[81] S. J. Godsill, A. Doucet, and M. West. 'Monte Carlo Smoothing for Nonlinear Time Series'. In: *Journal of the American Statistical Association* 99.465 (2004), pp. 156–168.

[82] S. Godsill, A. Doucet, and M. West. 'Maximum a Posteriori Sequence Estimation Using Monte Carlo Particle Filters'. In: *Annals of the Institute of Statistical Mathematics* 53.1 (2001), pp. 82–96.

[83] N. J. Gordon, D. J. Salmond, and A. F. M. Smith. 'Novel Approach to Nonlinear/non-Gaussian Bayesian State Estimation'. In: *IEE Proceedings F Radar and Signal Processing* 140.2 (1993), pp. 107–113.

[84] T. Górecki and M. Łuczak. 'Using Derivatives in Time Series Classification'. In: *Data Mining and Knowledge Discovery* 26.2 (2013), pp. 310–331.

[85] P. Gouverneur, J. Jaworek-Korjakowska, L. Köping, K. Shirahama, P. Kleczek, and M. Grzegorzek. 'Classification of Physiological Data for Emotion Recognition'. In: *Proceedings of the International Conference on Artificial Intelligence and Soft Computing.* 2017, pp. 619–627.

[86] B. Graham, C. Tachtatzis, F. Di Franco, M. Bykowski, D. C. Tracey, N. F. Timmons, and J. Morrison. 'Analysis of the Effect of Human Presence on a Wireless Sensor Network'. In: *International Journal of Ambient Computing and Intelligence* 3.1 (2011).

[87] E. L. Grand and S. Thrun. '3-Axis Magnetic Field Mapping and Fusion For Indoor Localization'. In: *Proceedings of the IEEE International Conference on Multisensor Fusion and Integration for Intelligent Systems.* 2012, pp. 358–364.

[88] K. W. Grant. 'The Effect of Speechreading on Masked Detection Thresholds for Filtered Speech'. In: *The Journal of the Acoustical Society of America* 109.5 (2001), pp. 2272–2275.

[89] K. W. Grant and P.-F. Seitz. 'The Use of Visible Speech Cues for Improving Auditory Detection of Spoken Sentences'. In: *The Journal of the Acoustical Society of America* 108.3 (2000), pp. 1197–1208.

[90] A. Greco, G. Valenza, and E. P. Scilingo. *Advances in Electrodermal Activity Processing with Applications for Mental Health: From Heuristic Methods to Convex Optimization.* 1st Edition. Cham, Switzerland: Springer Publishing Company, Incorporated, 2016.

[91] R. Guo, S. Li, L. He, W. Gao, H. Qi, and G. Owens. 'Pervasive and Unobtrusive Emotion Sensing for Human Mental Health'. In: *Proceedings of the 7th International Conference on Pervasive Computing Technologies for Healthcare and Workshops.* 2013, pp. 436–439.

[92] F. Gustafsson, F. Gunnarsson, N. Bergman, U. Forssell, J. Jansson, R. Karlsson, and P.-J. Nordlund. 'Particle Filters for Positioning, Navigation, and Tracking'. In: *IEEE Transactions on Signal Processing* 50.2 (2002), pp. 425–437.

[93] S. h. Fang, T. n. Lin, and K. c. Lee. 'A Novel Algorithm for Multipath Fingerprinting in Indoor WLAN Environments'. In: *IEEE Transactions on Wireless Communications* 7.9 (2008).

[94] S. Hagler, D. Austin, T. L. Hayes, J. Kaye, and M. Pavel. 'Unobtrusive and Ubiquitous In-Home Monitoring: A Methodology for Continuous Assessment of Gait Velocity in Elders'. In: *IEEE Transactions on Biomedical Engineering* 57.4 (2010), pp. 813–820.

[95] N. Y. Hammerla, S. Halloran, and T. Plötz. 'Deep, Convolutional, and Recurrent Models for Human Activity Recognition Using Wearables'. In: *Proceedings of the 25th International Joint Conference on Artificial Intelligence.* 2016, pp. 1533–1540.

[96] H. Hamooni and A. Mueen. 'Dual-Domain Hierarchical Classification of Phonetic Time Series'. In: *Proceedings of the IEEE International Conference on Data Mining*. 2014, pp. 160–169.

[97] R. Harle. 'A Survey of Indoor Inertial Positioning Systems for Pedestrians'. In: *IEEE Communications Surveys and Tutorials* 15.3 (2013), pp. 1281–1293.

[98] A. Harter and A. Hopper. 'A Distributed Location System for the Active Office'. In: *IEEE Network* 8.1 (1994), pp. 62–70.

[99] H. He and E. Garcia. 'Learning from Imbalanced Data'. In: *IEEE Transactions on Knowledge and Data Engineering* 21.9 (2009), pp. 1263–1284.

[100] S. He and S. H. G. Chan. 'Sectjunction: Wi-Fi Indoor Localization Based on Junction of Signal Sectors'. In: *Proceedings of the IEEE International Conference on Communications*. 2014, pp. 2605–2610.

[101] S. He and S. H. G. Chan. 'Wi-Fi Fingerprint-based Indoor Positioning: Recent Advances and Comparisons'. In: *IEEE Communications Surveys Tutorials* 18.1 (2016), pp. 466–490.

[102] S. Helal, W. Mann, H. El-Zabadani, J. King, Y. Kaddoura, and E. Jansen. 'The Gator Tech Smart House: A Programmable Pervasive Space'. In: *Computer* 38.3 (2005), pp. 50–60.

[103] S. Hilsenbeck, D. Bobkov, G. Schroth, R. Huitl, and E. Steinbach. 'Graph-based Data Fusion of Pedometer and WiFi Measurements for Mobile Indoor Positioning'. In: *Proceedings of the ACM International Joint Conference on Pervasive and Ubiquitous Computing*. 2014, pp. 147–158.

[104] G. Hinton, L. Deng, D. Yu, G. E. Dahl, A. r. Mohamed, N. Jaitly, A. Senior, V. Vanhoucke, P. Nguyen, T. N. Sainath, and B. Kingsbury. 'Deep Neural Networks for Acoustic Modeling in Speech Recognition: The Shared Views of Four Research Groups'. In: *IEEE Signal Processing Magazine* 29.6 (2012), pp. 82–97.

[105] S. Hoseinitabatabaei, A. Gluhak, and R. Tafazolli. 'uDirect: A Novel Approach for Pervasive Observation of User Direction with Mobile Phones'. In: *Proceedings of the IEEE International Conference on Pervasive Computing and Communications*. 2011, pp. 74–83.

[106] S. Hoseinitabatabaei, A. Gluhak, R. Tafazolli, and W. Headley. 'Design, Realization, and Evaluation of uDirect-An Approach for Pervasive Observation of User Facing Direction on Mobile Phones'. In: *IEEE Transactions on Mobile Computing* 13.9 (2014), pp. 1981–1994.

[107] D. H. Hu and Q. Yang. 'Transfer Learning for Activity Recognition via Sensor Mapping'. In: *Proceedings of the 22nd International Joint Conference on Artificial Intelligence - Volume 3*. 2011, pp. 1962–1967.

[108] E. J. Humphrey, J. P. Bello, and Y. LeCun. 'Feature Learning and Deep Architectures: New Directions For Music Informatics'. In: *Journal of Intelligent Information Systems* 41.3 (2013), pp. 461–481.

[109] S. S. Intille, K. Larson, E. M. Tapia, J. S. Beaudin, P. Kaushik, J. Nawyn, and R. Rockinson. 'Using a Live-in Laboratory for Ubiquitous Computing Research'. In: *Proceedings of the 4th International Conference on Pervasive Computing*. 2006, pp. 349–365.

[110] M. Isard and A. Blake. 'CONDENSATION - Conditional Density Propagation for Visual Tracking'. In: *International Journal of Computer Vision* 29.1 (1998), pp. 5–28.

[111] M. Isard and A. Blake. 'Contour Tracking by Stochastic Propagation of Conditional Density'. In: *Proceedings of the 4th European Conference on Computer Vision* 1 (1996), pp. 343–356.

[112] F. Itakura. 'Minimum Prediction Residual Principle Applied to Speech Recognition'. In: *IEEE Transactions on Acoustics, Speech, and Signal Processing* 23.1 (1975), pp. 67–72.

[113] D. J. Jacob. *Introduction to Atmospheric Chemistry*. Princeton, New Jersey, USA: Princeton University Press, 1999.

[114] A. K. Jain, R. P. W. Duin, and J. Mao. 'Statistical Pattern Recognition: A Review'. In: *IEEE Transactions on Pattern Analysis and Machine Intelligence* 22.1 (2000), pp. 4–37.

[115] Y.-S. Jeong, M. K. Jeong, and O. A. Omitaomu. 'Weighted Dynamic Time Warping For Time Series Classification'. In: *Pattern Recognition* 44.9 (2011), pp. 2231–2240.

[116] Y. Ji, S. Biaz, S. Pandey, and P. Agrawal. 'ARIADNE: A Dynamic Indoor Signal Map Construction and Localization System'. In: *Proceedings of the 4th International Conference on Mobile Systems, Applications and Services*. 2006, pp. 151–164.

[117] Y. G. Jiang, J. Yang, C. W. Ngo, and A. G. Hauptmann. 'Representations of Keypoint-Based Semantic Concept Detection: A Comprehensive Study'. In: *IEEE Transactions on Multimedia* 12.1 (2010), pp. 42–53.

[118] *JINS MEME: The world's first wearable eyewear that lets you see yourself.* https://jins-meme.com/en/. Accessed: 2018-04-05.

[119] W. R. Jung, S. Bell, A. Petrenko, and A. Sizo. 'Potential Risks of WiFi-based Indoor Positioning and Progress on Improving Localization Functionality'. In: *Proceedings of the 4th ACM SIGSPATIAL International Workshop on Indoor Spatial Awareness*. 2012, pp. 13–20.

[120] H. Junker, O. Amft, P. Lukowicz, and G. Tröster. 'Gesture Spotting with Body-worn Inertial Sensors to Detect User Activities'. In: *Pattern Recognition* 41.6 (2008), pp. 2010–2024.

[121] K. El-Kafrawy, M. Youssef, A. El-Keyi, and A. Naguib. 'Propagation Modeling for Accurate Indoor WLAN RSS-Based Localization'. In: *Proceedings of the 72nd IEEE Vehicular Technology Conference - Fall*. 2010, pp. 1–5.

[122] R. E. Kalman. 'A New Approach to Linear Filtering and Prediction Problems'. In: *Transactions of the ASME–Journal of Basic Engineering* 82.D (1960), pp. 35–45.

[123] W. Kang and Y. Han. 'SmartPDR: Smartphone-Based Pedestrian Dead Reckoning for Indoor Localization'. In: *IEEE Sensors Journal* 15.5 (2015), pp. 2906–2916.

[124] E. D. Kaplan and C. J. Hegarty. *Understanding GPS - Principles and Applications*. 2nd Edition. Norwood, MA, USA: Artech House, 2006.

[125] R. J. Kate. 'Using Dynamic Time Warping Distances as Features for Improved Time Series Classification'. In: *Data Mining and Knowledge Discovery* 30.2 (2016), pp. 283–312.

[126] C. Kayser and L. Shams. 'Multisensory Causal Inference in the Brain'. In: *PLoS Biology* 13.2 (2015), pp. 1–7.

[127] E. J. Keogh and M. J. Pazzani. 'A Simple Dimensionality Reduction Technique for Fast Similarity Search in Large Time Series Databases'. In: *Knowledge Discovery and Data Mining. Current Issues and New Applications*. 2000, pp. 122–133.

[128] E. Keogh, K. Chakrabarti, M. Pazzani, and S. Mehrotra. 'Locally Adaptive Dimensionality Reduction for Indexing Large Time Series Databases'. In: *SIGMOD Record* 30.2 (2001), pp. 151–162.

[129] A. Khalajmehrabadi, N. Gatsis, and D. Akopian. 'Modern WLAN Fingerprinting Indoor Positioning Methods and Deployment Challenges'. In: *IEEE Communications Surveys Tutorials* 19.3 (2017), pp. 1974–2002.

[130] D. H. Kim, K. Han, and D. Estrin. 'Employing User Feedback for Semantic Location Services'. In: *Proceedings of the 13th International Conference on Ubiquitous Computing*. 2011, pp. 217–226.

[131]   G. Kitagawa. 'Monte Carlo Filter and Smoother for non-Gaussian Nonlinear State Space Models'. In: *Journal of Computational and Graphical Statistics* 5.1 (1996), pp. 1–25.

[132]   A. Kong, J. S. Liu, and W. H. Wong. 'Sequential Imputations and Bayesian Missing Data Problems'. In: *Journal of the American Statistical Association* 89.425 (1994), pp. 278–288.

[133]   L. Köping, M. Grzegorzek, F. Deinzer, S. Bobek, M. Ślażyński, and G. J. Nalepa. 'Improving Indoor Localization by User Feedback'. In: *Proceedings of the 18th International Conference on Information Fusion*. 2015, pp. 1053–1060.

[134]   L. Köping, M. Grzegorzek, and F. Deinzer. 'Probabilistic Step and Turn Detection in Indoor Localization'. In: *Proceedings of the Conference on Data Fusion and Target Tracking: Algorithms and Applications*. 2014, pp. 1–7.

[135]   L. Köping, T. Mühsam, C. Ofenberg, B. Czech, M. Bernard, J. Schmer, and F. Deinzer. 'Indoor Navigation Using Particle Filter and Sensor Fusion'. In: *Annual of Navigation* 19.2 (2012), pp. 31–40.

[136]   L. Köping, K. Shirahama, and M. Grzegorzek. 'A General Framework For Sensor-based Human Activity Recognition'. In: *Computers in Biology and Medicine* 95 (2018), pp. 248–260.

[137]   K. Kunze and P. Lukowicz. 'Sensor Placement Variations in Wearable Activity Recognition'. In: *IEEE Pervasive Computing* 13.4 (Oct. 2014), pp. 32–41.

[138]   K. Kunze, P. Lukowicz, K. Partridge, and B. Begole. 'Which Way Am I Facing: Inferring Horizontal Device Orientation from an Accelerometer Signal'. In: *Proceedings of the International Symposium on Wearable Computers*. 2009, pp. 149–150.

[139]   K. Kunze and P. Lukowicz. 'Dealing with Sensor Displacement in Motion-based Onbody Activity Recognition Systems'. In: *Proceedings of the 10th International Conference on Ubiquitous Computing*. 2008, pp. 20–29.

[140]   A. LaMarca, Y. Chawathe, S. Consolvo, J. Hightower, I. Smith, J. Scott, T. Sohn, J. Howard, J. Hughes, F. Potter, J. Tabert, P. Powledge, G. Borriello, and B. Schilit. 'Place Lab: Device Positioning Using Radio Beacons in the Wild'. In: *Proceedings of the 3rd International Conference on Pervasive Computing*. 2005, pp. 116–133.

[141]   M. Längkvist, L. Karlsson, and A. Loutfi. 'A Review of Unsupervised Feature Learning and Deep Learning for Time-series Modeling'. In: *Pattern Recognition Letters* 42.Supplement C (2014), pp. 11–24.

[142] O. D. Lara and M. A. Labrador. 'A Survey on Human Activity Recognition using Wearable Sensors'. In: *IEEE Communications Surveys Tutorials* 15.3 (2013), pp. 1192–1209.

[143] Y. LeCun, Y. Bengio, and G. Hinton. 'Deep Learning'. In: *Nature* 521.7553 (2015), pp. 436–444.

[144] H. Leppäkoski, S. Tikkinen, and J. Takala. 'Optimizing Radio Map for WLAN Fingerprinting'. In: *Proceedings of the Ubiquitous Positioning Indoor Navigation and Location Based Service*. 2010.

[145] B. Li, T. Gallagher, A. G. Dempster, and C. Rizos. 'How Feasible is the Use of Magnetic Field Alone for Indoor Positioning?' In: *Proceedings of the International Conference on Indoor Positioning and Indoor Navigation*. 2012, pp. 1–9.

[146] B. Li, B. Harvey, and T. Gallagher. 'Using Barometers to Determine the Height for Indoor Positioning'. In: *Proceedings of the International Conference on Indoor Positioning and Indoor Navigation*. 2013, pp. 1–7.

[147] F. Li, C. Zhao, G. Ding, J. Gong, C. Liu, and F. Zhao. 'A Reliable and Accurate Indoor Localization Method Using Phone Inertial Sensors'. In: *Proceedings of the ACM Conference on Ubiquitous Computing*. 2012, pp. 421–430.

[148] F. Li, L. Köping, S. Schmitz, and M. Grzegorzek. 'Real-Time Gesture Recognition using a Particle Filtering Approach'. In: *Proceedings of the 6th International Conference on Pattern Recognition Applications and Methods*. 2017, pp. 394–401.

[149] L. Liao, D. Fox, J. Hightower, H. Kautz, and D. Schulz. 'Voronoi Tracking: Location Estimation Using Sparse and Noisy Sensor Data'. In: *Proceedings of the IEEE/RSJ International Conference on Intelligent Robots and Systems*. 2003, 723–728 vol.1.

[150] J. Lin, E. Keogh, S. Lonardi, and B. Chiu. 'A Symbolic Representation of Time Series, with Implications for Streaming Algorithms'. In: *Proceedings of the 8th ACM SIGMOD Workshop on Research Issues in Data Mining and Knowledge Discovery*. 2003, pp. 2–11.

[151] J. Lin, E. Keogh, L. Wei, and S. Lonardi. 'Experiencing SAX: A Novel Symbolic Representation of Time Series'. In: *Data Mining and Knowledge Discovery* 15.2 (2007), pp. 107–144.

[152] J. Lin, R. Khade, and Y. Li. 'Rotation-invariant Similarity in Time Series Using Bag-of-patterns Representation'. In: *Journal of Intelligent Information Systems* 39.2 (2012), pp. 287–315.

[153] J. A. B. Link, P. Smith, and K. Wehrle. 'FootPath: Accurate Map-based Indoor Navigation Using Smartphones'. In: *Proceedings of the International Conference on Indoor Positioning and Indoor Navigation*. 2011, pp. 1–8.

[154] H. Liu, H. Darabi, P. Banerjee, and J. Liu. 'Survey of Wireless Indoor Positioning Techniques and Systems'. In: *IEEE Transactions on Systems, Man, and Cybernetics, Part C (Applications and Reviews)* 37.6 (2007).

[155] H. Liu, Y. Gan, J. Yang, S. Sidhom, Y. Wang, Y. Chen, and F. Ye. 'Push the Limit of WiFi Based Localization for Smartphones'. In: *Proceedings of the 18th Annual International Conference on Mobile Computing and Networking*. 2012.

[156] J. Liu, L. Zhong, J. Wickramasuriya, and V. Vasudevan. 'uWave: Accelerometer-based Personalized Gesture Recognition and Its Applications'. In: *Pervasive Mobile Computing* 5.6 (2009), pp. 657–675.

[157] J. S. Liu and R. Chen. 'Sequential Monte Carlo Methods for Dynamic Systems'. In: *Journal of the American Statistical Association* 93.443 (1998), pp. 1032–1044.

[158] B. Logan, J. Healey, M. Philipose, E. M. Tapia, and S. Intille. 'A Long-term Evaluation of Sensing Modalities for Activity Recognition'. In: *Proceedings of the 9th International Conference on Ubiquitous Computing*. 2007.

[159] Y. Luo, Y. Chen, and O. Hoeber. 'Wi-Fi-Based Indoor Positioning Using Human-Centric Collaborative Feedback'. In: *Proceedings of the IEEE International Conference on Communications*. 2011.

[160] A. K. M. Mahtab Hossain, H. Nguyen Van, and W.-S. Soh. 'Utilization of User Feedback in Indoor Positioning System'. In: *Pervasive and Mobile Computing* 6.4 (2010), pp. 467–481.

[161] C. D. Manning, P. Raghavan, and H. Schütze. *Introduction to Information Retrieval*. New York, NY, USA: Cambridge University Press, 2008.

[162] M. Marschollek, M. Goevercin, K.-H. Wolf, B. Song, M. Gietzelt, R. Haux, and E. Steinhagen-Thiessen. 'A Performance Comparison of Accelerometry-based Step Detection Algorithms on a Large, Non-laboratory Sample of Healthy and Mobility-impaired Persons'. In: *Proceedings of the 30th Annual International Conference of the IEEE on Engineering in Medicine and Biology Society*. 2008, pp. 1319–1322.

[163] H. P. Martinez, Y. Bengio, and G. N. Yannakakis. 'Learning Deep Physiological Models of Affect'. In: *IEEE Computational Intelligence Magazine* 8.2 (2013), pp. 20–33.

[164] W. Meng, W. Xiao, W. Ni, and L. Xie. *Secure and Robust Wi-Fi Fingerprinting Indoor Localization*. 2011.

[165] *Microsoft Band.* https://www.microsoft.com/en-us/band. Accessed: 2018-04-05.

[166] S. Mitra and T. Acharya. 'Gesture Recognition: A Survey'. In: *IEEE Transactions on Systems, Man, and Cybernetics, Part C (Applications and Reviews)* 37.3 (2007), pp. 311–324.

[167] D. Mizell. 'Using Gravity to Estimate Accelerometer Orientation'. In: *Proceedings of the 7th IEEE International Symposium on Wearable Computers.* 2003, pp. 252–253.

[168] N. Mohssen, R. Momtaz, H. Aly, and M. Youssef. 'It's the Human That Matters: Accurate User Orientation Estimation for Mobile Computing Applications'. In: *Proceedings of the 11th International Conference on Mobile and Ubiquitous Systems: Computing, Networking and Services.* 2014, pp. 70–79.

[169] D. Molkdar. 'Review on Radio Propagation into and Within Buildings'. In: *IEE Proceedings H - Microwaves, Antennas and Propagation* 138.1 (1991), pp. 61–73.

[170] F. J. O. Morales and D. Roggen. 'Deep Convolutional Feature Transfer Across Mobile Activity Recognition Domains, Sensor Modalities and Locations'. In: *Proceedings of the ACM International Symposium on Wearable Computers.* 2016, pp. 92–99.

[171] F. Mörchen. *Time Series Feature Extraction for Data Mining Using DWT and DFT.* Tech. rep. 33. Department of Mathematics and Computer Science, Philipps-University Marburg, 2003.

[172] F. Mörchen. 'Time Series Knowledge Mining'. PhD thesis. Philipps-University Marburg, 2006.

[173] A. Mueen and E. Keogh. 'Extracting Optimal Performance from Dynamic Time Warping'. In: *Proceedings of the 22nd ACM SIGKDD International Conference on Knowledge Discovery and Data Mining.* 2016, pp. 2129–2130.

[174] M. Müller, D. P. W. Ellis, A. Klapuri, and G. Richard. 'Signal Processing for Music Analysis'. In: *IEEE Journal of Selected Topics in Signal Processing* 5.6 (2011), pp. 1088–1110.

[175] M. Müller. In: *Information Retrieval for Music and Motion.* Berlin, Heidelberg: Springer, 2007. Chap. Dynamic Time Warping, pp. 69–84.

[176] K. Murphy. *Machine Learning: A Probabilistic Perspective.* Cambridge, MA: The MIT Press, 2012.

[177] A. Nanopoulos, R. Alcock, and Y. Manolopoulos. 'Information Processing and Technology'. In: ed. by N. Mastorakis and S. D. Nikolopoulos. Commack, NY, USA: Nova Science Publishers, Inc., 2001. Chap. Feature-based Classification of Time-series Data, pp. 49–61.

[178] A. Neskovic, N. Neskovic, and G. Paunovic. 'Modern Approaches in Modeling of Mobile Radio Systems Propagation Environment'. In: *IEEE Communications Surveys Tutorials* 3.3 (2000), pp. 2–12.

[179] L. T. Nguyen and J. Zhang. 'Wi-Fi Fingerprinting Through Active Learning Using Smartphones'. In: *Proceedings of the ACM Conference on Pervasive and Ubiquitous Computing Adjunct Publication*. 2013, pp. 969–976.

[180] C. Nickel, H. Brandt, and C. Busch. 'Benchmarking the Performance of SVMs and HMMs for Accelerometer-based Biometric Gait Recognition'. In: *Proceedings of the IEEE International Symposium on Signal Processing and Information Technology*. 2011, pp. 281–286.

[181] H. Niemann. *Klassifikation von Mustern*. 2nd Edition. Berlin Heidelberg: Springer, 2003.

[182] E. Nowak, F. Jurie, and B. Triggs. 'Sampling Strategies for Bag-of-features Image Classification'. In: *Proceedings of the 9th European Conference on Computer Vision - Volume Part IV*. 2006, pp. 490–503.

[183] H. Nurminen, A. Ristimaki, S. Ali-Loytty, and R. Piche. 'Particle Filter and Smoother for Indoor Localization'. In: *Proceedings of the International Conference on Indoor Positioning and Indoor Navigation*. 2013, pp. 1–10.

[184] H. Nurminen, M. Koivisto, S. Ali-Löytty, and R. Piché. 'Motion Model for Positioning with Graph-Based Indoor Map'. In: *Proceedings of the International Conference on Indoor Positioning and Indoor Navigation*. 2014, pp. 1–10.

[185] F. Ofli, R. Chaudhry, G. Kurillo, R. Vidal, and R. Bajcsy. 'Berkeley MHAD: A comprehensive Multimodal Human Action Database'. In: *IEEE Workshop on Applications of Computer Vision*. 2013, pp. 53–60.

[186] H. op den Akker, V. M. Jones, and H. J. Hermens. 'Tailoring Real-time Physical Activity Coaching Systems: A Literature Survey and Model'. In: *User Modeling and User-Adapted Interaction* 24.5 (2014), pp. 351–392.

[187] P. Ordonez, T. Armstrong, T. Oates, and J. Fackler. 'Using Modified Multivariate Bag-of-Words Models to Classify Physiological Data'. In: *Proceedings of the 11th IEEE International Conference on Data Mining Workshops*. 2011, pp. 534–539.

[188] V. N. P. P. Bahl and A. Balachandran. *Enhancements to the RADAR User Location and Tracking System*. Tech. rep. MSR-TR-2000-12. Microsoft Research, 2000.

[189] S. J. Pan and Q. Yang. 'A Survey on Transfer Learning'. In: *IEEE Transactions on Knowledge and Data Engineering* 22.10 (2010), pp. 1345–1359.

[190] S. J. Pan, J. T. Kwok, Q. Yang, and J. J. Pan. 'Adaptive Localization in a Dynamic WiFi Environment Through Multi-view Learning'. In: *Proceedings of the 22nd National Conference on Artificial Intelligence - Volume 2*. 2007, pp. 1108–1113.

[191] A. Parameswaran, A. D. Sarma, H. Garcia-Molina, N. Polyzotis, and J. Widom. 'Human-assisted Graph Search: It's Okay to Ask Questions'. In: *Proceedings of the VLDB Endowment* 4.5 (2011), pp. 267–278.

[192] M. Pedley. *Tilt Sensing Using a Three-Axis Accelerometer*. Tech. rep. AN3461. Freescale Semiconductor, 2013.

[193] F. Perronnin, J. Sánchez, and T. Mensink. 'Improving the Fisher Kernel for Large-scale Image Classification'. In: *Proceedings of the 11th European Conference on Computer Vision: Part IV*. 2010, pp. 143–156.

[194] F. Petitjean, G. Forestier, G. I. Webb, A. E. Nicholson, Y. Chen, and E. Keogh. 'Dynamic Time Warping Averaging of Time Series Allows Faster and More Accurate Classification'. In: *2014 IEEE International Conference on Data Mining*. Dec. 2014, pp. 470–479.

[195] F. Petitjean, A. Ketterlin, and P. Gançarski. 'A Global Averaging Method for Dynamic Time Warping, with Applications to Clustering'. In: *Pattern Recognition* 44.3 (2011), pp. 678–693.

[196] M. Philipose, K. P. Fishkin, M. Perkowitz, D. J. Patterson, D. Fox, H. Kautz, and D. Hahnel. 'Inferring Activities From Interactions With Objects'. In: *IEEE Pervasive Computing* 3.4 (2004), pp. 50–57.

[197] A. Phinyomark, P. Phukpattaranont, and C. Limsakul. 'Feature Reduction and Selection for EMG Signal Classification'. In: *Expert Systems with Applications* 39.8 (2012), pp. 7420–7431.

[198] R. W. Picard, E. Vyzas, and J. Healey. 'Toward Machine Emotional Intelligence: Analysis of Affective Physiological State'. In: *IEEE Transactions on Pattern Analysis and Machine Intelligence* 23.10 (2001), pp. 1175–1191.

[199] M. K. Pitt and N. Shephard. 'Filtering Via Simulation: Auxiliary Particle Filters'. In: *Journal of the American Statistical Association* 94.446 (1999), pp. 590–599.

[200] T. Plötz, N. Y. Hammerla, and P. Olivier. 'Feature Learning for Activity Recognition in Ubiquitous Computing'. In: *Proceedings of the 22th International Joint Conference on Artificial Intelligence*. 2011, pp. 1729–1734.

[201] I. Popivanov and R. J. Miller. 'Similarity Search Over Time-series Data Using Wavelets'. In: *Proceedings of the 18th International Conference on Data Engineering*. 2002, pp. 212–221.

[202] N. B. Priyantha, A. Chakraborty, and H. Balakrishnan. 'The Cricket Location-support System'. In: *Proceedings of the 6th Annual International Conference on Mobile Computing and Networking*. 2000, pp. 32–43.

[203] *RabbitMQ - Messaging that just works*. https://www.rabbitmq.com/. Accessed: 2018-03-13.

[204] L. R. Rabiner. 'A Tutorial on Hidden Markov Models and Selected Applications in Speech Recognition'. In: *Proceedings of the IEEE* 77.2 (1989), pp. 257–286.

[205] V. Radu, N. D. Lane, S. Bhattacharya, C. Mascolo, M. K. Marina, and F. Kawsar. 'Towards Multimodal Deep Learning for Activity Recognition on Mobile Devices'. In: *Proceedings of the ACM International Joint Conference on Pervasive and Ubiquitous Computing: Adjunct*. 2016, pp. 185–188.

[206] D. Rafiei and A. O. Mendelzon. 'Querying Time Series Data Based on Similarity'. In: *IEEE Transactions on Knowledge and Data Engineering* 12.5 (2000), pp. 675–693.

[207] A. Rai, K. K. Chintalapudi, V. N. Padmanabhan, and R. Sen. 'Zee: Zero-effort Crowdsourcing for Indoor Localization'. In: *Proceedings of the 18th Annual International Conference on Mobile Computing and Networking*. 2012, pp. 293–304.

[208] T. Rakthanmanon, B. Campana, A. Mueen, G. Batista, B. Westover, Q. Zhu, J. Zakaria, and E. Keogh. 'Searching and Mining Trillions of Time Series Subsequences Under Dynamic Time Warping'. In: *Proceedings of the 18th ACM SIGKDD International Conference on Knowledge Discovery and Data Mining*. 2012, pp. 262–270.

[209] T. Rappaport. *Wireless Communications: Principles and Practice*. 2nd. Upper Saddle River, NJ, USA: Prentice Hall PTR, 2002.

[210] T. M. Rath and R. Manmatha. 'Word Image Matching Using Dynamic Time Warping'. In: *Proceedings of the IEEE Computer Society Conference on Computer Vision and Pattern Recognition*. Vol. 2. 2003, pp. 521–527.

[211] S. S. Rautaray and A. Agrawal. 'Vision Based Hand Gesture Recognition for Human Computer Interaction: A Survey'. In: *Artificial Intelligence Review* 43.1 (2015), pp. 1–54.

[212] T. Roos, P. Myllymäki, H. Tirri, P. Misikangas, and J. Sievänen. 'A Probabilistic Approach to WLAN User Location Estimation'. In: *International Journal of Wireless Information Networks* 9.3 (2002), pp. 155–164.

[213] K. Saeed, M. Tabędzki, M. Rybnik, and M. Adamski. 'K3M: A Universal Algorithm for Image Skeletonization and a Review of Thinning Techniques'. In: *International Journal of Applied Mathematics and Computer Science* 20.2 (2010), pp. 317–335.

[214] N. Saito. 'Local Feature Extraction and Its Application Using a Library of Bases'. PhD thesis. Yale University, 1994.

[215] H. Sakoe and S. Chiba. 'Dynamic Programming Algorithm Optimization for Spoken Word Recognition'. In: *IEEE Transactions on Acoustics, Speech, and Signal Processing* 26.1 (1978), pp. 43–49.

[216] S. Särkkä. *Bayesian Filtering and Smoothing*. 3rd Edition. Cambridge, United Kingdom: Cambridge University Press, 2014.

[217] J.-L. Schwartz, F. Berthommier, and C. Savariaux. 'Seeing to Hear Better: Evidence for Early Audio-visual Interactions in Speech Identification'. In: *Cognition* 93.2 (2004), B69–B78.

[218] S. Y. Seidel and T. S. Rappaport. '914 MHz Path Loss Prediction Models for Indoor Wireless Communications in Multifloored Buildings'. In: *IEEE Transactions on Antennas and Propagation* 40.2 (1992), pp. 207–217.

[219] P. Senin and S. Malinchik. 'SAX-VSM: Interpretable Time Series Classification Using SAX and Vector Space Model'. In: *Proceedings of the 13th IEEE International Conference on Data Mining*. 2013, pp. 1175–1180.

[220] J. S. Seybold. *Introduction to RF Propagation*. Hoboken, New Jersey, USA: John Wiley & Sons, 2005.

[221] H. Shatkay and S. B. Zdonik. 'Approximate Queries and Representations for Large Data Sequences'. In: *Proceedings of the 12th International Conference on Data Engineering*. 1996, pp. 536–545.

[222] K. Shirahama, L. Köping, and M. Grzegorzek. 'Codebook Approach for Sensor-based Human Activity Recognition'. In: *Proceedings of the ACM International Joint Conference on Pervasive and Ubiquitous Computing*. 2016, pp. 197–200.

[223]   K. Shirahama, Y. Matsuoka, and K. Uehara. 'Hybrid Negative Example Selection Using Visual and Conceptual Features'. In: *Multimedia Tools and Applications* 71.3 (2014), pp. 967–989.

[224]   K. Shirahama and K. Uehara. 'Kobe University and Muroran Institute of Technology at TRECVID 2012 Semantic Indexing Task'. In: *Proceedings of TRECVID.* 2012, pp. 239–247.

[225]   I. Skog, P. Handel, J. O. Nilsson, and J. Rantakokko. 'Zero-Velocity Detection - An Algorithm Evaluation'. In: *IEEE Transactions on Biomedical Engineering* 57.11 (2010), pp. 2657–2666.

[226]   C. G. M. Snoek, M. Worring, and A. W. M. Smeulders. 'Early Versus Late Fusion in Semantic Video Analysis'. In: *Proceedings of the 13th Annual ACM International Conference on Multimedia.* 2005, pp. 399–402.

[227]   U. Steinhoff and B. Schiele. 'Dead Reckoning From the Pocket - An Experimental Study'. In: *Proceedings of the IEEE International Conference on Pervasive Computing and Communications.* 2010, pp. 162–170.

[228]   B. L. R. Stojkoska and K. V. Trivodaliev. 'A Review of Internet of Things For Smart Home: Challenges and Solutions'. In: *Journal of Cleaner Production* 140 (2017), pp. 1454–1464.

[229]   S. Theodoridis and K. Koutroumbas. *Pattern Recognition.* 4th Edition. Burlington, MA, USA: Academic Press, 2009.

[230]   S. Thrun, W. Burgard, and D. Fox. *Probabilistic Robotics.* Cambridge, MA, USA: MIT Press, 2005.

[231]   Q. Tian, Z. Salcic, K. I. K. Wang, and Y. Pan. 'A Multi-Mode Dead Reckoning System for Pedestrian Tracking Using Smartphones'. In: *IEEE Sensors Journal* 16.7 (2016), pp. 2079–2093.

[232]   D. Titterton and J. Weston. *Strapdown Inertial Navigation Technology.* American Institute of Aeronautics and Astronautics, 2004.

[233]   A. Vakanski, I. Mantegh, A. Irish, and F. Janabi-Sharifi. 'Trajectory Learning for Robot Programming by Demonstration Using Hidden Markov Model and Dynamic Time Warping'. In: *IEEE Transactions on Systems, Man, and Cybernetics, Part B (Cybernetics)* 42.4 (2012), pp. 1039–1052.

[234]   K. Van Laerhoven and K. Aidoo. 'Teaching Context to Applications'. In: *Personal and Ubiquitous Computing* 5.1 (2001), pp. 46–49.

[235]   J. C. van Gemert, C. J. Veenman, A. W. M. Smeulders, and J.-M. Geusebroek. 'Visual Word Ambiguity'. In: *IEEE Transactions on Pattern Analysis and Machine Intelligence* 32.7 (2010), pp. 1271–1283.

[236] T. L. M. van Kasteren, G. Englebienne, and B. J. A. Kröse. 'Transferring Knowledge of Activity Recognition Across Sensor Networks'. In: *Proceedings of the 8th International Conference on Pervasive Computing*. 2010, pp. 283–300.

[237] T. van Kasteren, A. Noulas, G. Englebienne, and B. Kröse. 'Accurate Activity Recognition in a Home Setting'. In: *Proceedings of the 10th International Conference on Ubiquitous Computing*. 2008.

[238] V. N. Vapnik. *The Nature of Statistical Learning Theory*. New York, NY, USA: Springer, 1995.

[239] S. Vinoski. 'Advanced Message Queuing Protocol'. In: *IEEE Internet Computing* 10.6 (2006), pp. 87–89.

[240] B. Wang, Q. Chen, L. T. Yang, and H. C. Chao. 'Indoor Smartphone Localization Via Fingerprint Crowdsourcing: Challenges and Approaches'. In: *IEEE Wireless Communications* 23.3 (2016), pp. 82–89.

[241] B. Wang, S. Zhou, W. Liu, and Y. Mo. 'Indoor Localization Based on Curve Fitting and Location Search Using Received Signal Strength'. In: *IEEE Transactions on Industrial Electronics* 62.1 (2015), pp. 572–582.

[242] H. Wang, S. Sen, A. Elgohary, M. Farid, M. Youssef, and R. R. Choudhury. 'No Need to War-drive: Unsupervised Indoor Localization'. In: *Proceedings of the 10th International Conference on Mobile Systems, Applications, and Services*. 2012, pp. 197–210.

[243] H. Wang, H. Lenz, A. Szabo, U. D. Hanebeck, and J. Bamberger. 'Fusion of Barometric Sensors, WLAN Signals and Building Information for 3-D Indoor/Campus Localization'. In: *In proceedings of International Conference on Multisensor Fusion and Integration for Intelligent Systems (MFI 2006)*. 2006, pp. 426–432.

[244] J. Wang, J. Yang, K. Yu, F. Lv, T. Huang, and Y. Gong. 'Locality-constrained Linear Coding for Image Classification'. In: *IEEE Computer Society Conference on Computer Vision and Pattern Recognition*. 2010, pp. 3360–3367.

[245] J. Wang, Q. Gao, H. Wang, H. Chen, and M. Jin. 'Differential Radio Map-based Robust Indoor Localization'. In: *Journal on Wireless Communications and Networking* 2011.17 (2011), pp. 1–12.

[246] J. Wang, P. Liu, M. F. She, S. Nahavandi, and A. Kouzani. 'Bag-of-words Representation for Biomedical Time Series Classification'. In: *Biomedical Signal Processing and Control* 8.6 (2013), pp. 634–644.

[247] J. Wang, P. Liu, M. F. She, S. Nahavandi, and A. Kouzani. 'Bag-of-words Representation for Biomedical Time Series Classification'. In: *Biomedical Signal Processing and Control* 8.6 (2013), pp. 634–644.

[248] X. Wang, K. Smith, and R. Hyndman. 'Characteristic-Based Clustering for Time Series Data'. In: *Data Mining and Knowledge Discovery* 13.3 (2006), pp. 335–364.

[249] R. Want and A. Hopper. 'Active Badges and Personal Interactive Computing Objects'. In: *IEEE Transactions on Consumer Electronics* 38.1 (1992), pp. 10–20.

[250] R. Want, A. Hopper, V. Falcão, and J. Gibbons. 'The Active Badge Location System'. In: *ACM Transactions on Information Systems* 10.1 (Jan. 1992), pp. 91–102.

[251] J. A. Ward, P. Lukowicz, and G. Tröster. 'Gesture Spotting Using Wrist Worn Microphone and 3-axis Accelerometer'. In: *Proceedings of the Joint Conference on Smart Objects and Ambient Intelligence: Innovative Context-aware Services: Usages and Technologies*. 2005, pp. 99–104.

[252] H. Weinberg. *Using the ADXL202 in Pedometer and Personal Navigation Applications*. Tech. rep. AN-602 Application Note. Analog Devices, 2002.

[253] M. Weiser. 'The Computer for the 21st Century'. In: *ACM SIGMOBILE Mobile Computing and Communications Review - Special issue dedicated to Mark Weiser* 3.3 (July 1999), pp. 3–11.

[254] G. Wiederhold. 'Mediators in the Architecture of Future Information Systems'. In: *Computer* 25.3 (1992), pp. 38–49.

[255] O. Woodman and R. Harle. 'Pedestrian Localisation for Indoor Environments'. In: *Proceedings of the 10th International Conference on Ubiquitous Computing* (2008), pp. 114–123.

[256] C. Wu, Z. Yang, and Y. Liu. 'Smartphones Based Crowdsourcing for Indoor Localization'. In: *IEEE Transactions on Mobile Computing* 14.2 (2015), pp. 444–457.

[257] J. Xiao, Z. Zhou, Y. Yi, and L. M. Ni. 'A Survey on Wireless Indoor Localization from the Device Perspective'. In: *ACM Computing Surveys* 49.2 (2016), 25:1–25:31.

[258] H. Xie, T. Gu, X. Tao, H. Ye, and J. Lu. 'A Reliability-Augmented Particle Filter for Magnetic Fingerprinting Based Indoor Localization on Smartphone'. In: *IEEE Transactions on Mobile Computing* 15.8 (2016), pp. 1877–1892.

[259] Q. Yang and X. Wu. '10 Challenging Problems in Data Mining Research'. In: *International Journal of Information Technology and Decision Making* 5.4 (2006), pp. 597–604.

[260] S. Yang and Q. Li. 'Ambulatory Walking Speed Estimation Under Different Step Lengths and Frequencies'. In: *2010 IEEE/ASME International Conference on Advanced Intelligent Mechatronics*. 2010, pp. 658–663.

[261] Z. Yang, C. Wu, and Y. Liu. 'Locating in Fingerprint Space: Wireless Indoor Localization with Little Human Intervention'. In: *Proceedings of the 18th Annual International Conference on Mobile Computing and Networking*. 2012, pp. 269–280.

[262] A. Yassin, Y. Nasser, M. Awad, A. Al-Dubai, R. Liu, C. Yuen, R. Raulefs, and E. Aboutanios. 'Recent Advances in Indoor Localization: A Survey on Theoretical Approaches and Applications'. In: *IEEE Communications Surveys Tutorials* 19.2 (2017), pp. 1327–1346.

[263] M. Youssef and A. Agrawala. 'The Horus WLAN Location Determination System'. In: *Proceedings of the 3rd International Conference on Mobile Systems, Applications, and Services*. 2005, pp. 205–218.

[264] J. Zhang, M. Marszalek, S. Lazebnik, and C. Schmid. 'Local Features and Kernels for Classification of Texture and Object Categories: A Comprehensive Study'. In: *International Journal of Computer Vision* 73.2 (2007), pp. 213–238.

[265] X. Zhou, K. Yu, T. Zhang, and T. S. Huang. 'Image Classification Using Supervector Coding of Local Image Descriptors'. In: *Proceedings of the 11th European Conference on Computer Vision: Part V*. 2010, pp. 141–154.

[266] Y. Zhuang, J. Yang, Y. Li, L. Qi, and N. El-Sheimy. 'Smartphone-based Indoor Localization with Bluetooth Low Energy Beacons'. In: *Sensors* 16.5 (2016), pp. 1–20.

In der Reihe *Studien zur Mustererkennung,*
herausgegeben von
Prof. Dr.-Ing Heinricht Niemann und Herrn Prof. Dr.-Ing. Elmar Nöth
sind bisher erschienen:

| 1 | Jürgen Haas | Probabilistic Methods in Linguistic Analysis |
| | | ISBN 978-3-89722-565-7, 2000, 260 S. 40.50 € |

| 2 | Manuela Boros | Partielles robustes Parsing spontansprachlicher Dialoge am Beispiel von Zugauskunftdialogen |
| | | ISBN 978-3-89722-600-5, 2001, 264 S. 40.50 € |

| 3 | Stefan Harbeck | Automatische Verfahren zur Sprachdetektion, Landessprachenerkennung und Themendetektion |
| | | ISBN 978-3-89722-766-8, 2001, 260 S. 40.50 € |

| 4 | Julia Fischer | Ein echtzeitfähiges Dialogsystem mit iterativer Ergebnisoptimierung |
| | | ISBN 978-3-89722-867-2, 2002, 222 S. 40.50 € |

| 5 | Ulrike Ahlrichs | Wissensbasierte Szenenexploration auf der Basis erlernter Analysestrategien |
| | | ISBN 978-3-89722-904-4, 2002, 165 S. 40.50 € |

| 6 | Florian Gallwitz | Integrated Stochastic Models for Spontaneous Speech Recognition |
| | | ISBN 978-3-89722-907-5, 2002, 196 S. 40.50 € |

| 7 | Uwe Ohler | Computational Promoter Recognition in Eukaryotic Genomic DNA |
| | | ISBN 978-3-89722-988-4, 2002, 206 S. 40.50 € |

| 8 | Richard Huber | Prosodisch-linguistische Klassifikation von Emotion |
| | | ISBN 978-3-89722-984-6, 2002, 293 S. 40.50 € |

39	Chen Li	Content-based Microscopic Image Analysis	
		ISBN 978-3-8325-4253-5, 2016, 196 S.	36.50 €
40	Christian Feinen	Object Representation and Matching Based on Skeletons and Curves	
		ISBN 978-3-8325-4257-3, 2016, 260 S.	50.50 €
41	Juan Rafael Orozco-Arroyave	Analysis of Speech of People with Parkinson's Disease	
		ISBN 978-3-8325-4361-7, 2016, 138 S.	38.00 €
42	Cong Yang	Object Shape Generation, Representation and Matching	
		ISBN 978-3-8325-4399-0, 2016, 194 S.	36.50 €
43	Florian Hönig	Automatic Assessment of Prosody in Second Language Learning	
		ISBN 978-3-8325-4567-3, 2017, 256 S.	38.50 €
44	Zeyd Boukhers	3D Trajectory Extraction from 2D Videos for Human Activity Analysis	
		ISBN 978-3-8325-4583-3, 2017, 152 S.	35.00 €
45	Muhammad Hassan Khan	Human Activity Analysis in Visual Surveillance and Healthcare	
		ISBN 978-3-8325-4807-0, 2018, 156 S.	35.00 €
46	Lukas Köping	Probabilistic Fusion of Multiple Distributed Sensors	
		ISBN 978-3-8325-4827-8, 2018, 170 S.	46.50 €

Alle erschienenen Bücher können unter der angegebenen ISBN im Buchhandel oder direkt beim Logos Verlag Berlin (www.logos-verlag.de, Fax: 030 - 42 85 10 92) bestellt werden.